NOTES

including
- *Life and Background*
- *Chronology of Plath*
- *Introduction to the Novel*
- *List of Characters*
- *Critical Commentaries*
- *Character Analyses*
- *Critical Essays*
  - Plath, the Individual, versus Society
  - What Went Wrong for Sylvia Plath?
  - Anxiety About Death in *The Bell Jar*
  - Suicide – A Conclusion
- *Essay Questions*
- *Select Bibliography*
- *Additional Readings*

by
Jeanne Inness, Ph.D.
Associate Professor, Daley College

INCORPORATED

LINCOLN, NEBRASKA 68501

Editor

Gary Carey, M.A.
University of Colorado

Consulting Editor

James L. Roberts, Ph.D.
Department of English
University of Nebraska

Cliffs Notes, Inc.   Lincoln, Nebraska

CONTENTS

THE BELL JAR NOTES

LIFE AND BACKGROUND

The first critical issue to confront the reader of *The Bell Jar* is the problem of classifying the book. Is this book really a novel? It is presented in the form of a long fictional work. Nevertheless, one might argue that the flatness of all the minor characters, plus the inability of the major character, Esther Greenwood, to come to any real dramatic resolution of her problems makes the work a second-rate piece of fiction – if indeed this is fiction at all. Hailed as an important literary work because it takes a liberated view of the plight of the modern American woman is not justification for calling this book a great, or even a good, work of art. Good social commentary or good narrative description of a problem is not necessarily art. This work, in fact, is a good example of what John Barth says of most contemporary women's fiction: "secular news reports."

So if *The Bell Jar* is fiction of questionable quality or even, questionably, fiction, how does one label the book? First, the reader should have some idea about the life of the author, Sylvia Plath. For example, one should know that Plath is best recognized for her poetry and also that she committed suicide when she was thirty. Reading about Plath's life makes it clear that in *The Bell Jar*, originally published under the pseudonym of Victoria Lucas, Plath was recording much of her personal experience, very lightly veiled as fiction. Plath attended Smith College and went to New York City in her junior year as a winner of a *Mademoiselle* writing contest; she tried to commit suicide with an overdose of sleeping pills, and she was hospitalized before finally finishing college. So is this book really just a documentary of Plath's college years? If so, why did she present it as fiction? Wouldn't the mental hospital scenes have had more power to change things if they had been presented as the real experiences of an accomplished female poet? These and other questions can never be satisfactorily answered. What we have, then, is a book about a certain era, published in a certain guise. Perhaps that is commentary enough on Sylvia Plath's life, her historical situation as an adolescent in the early 1950s, and commentary enough on her major piece of fiction.

The next issue that the reader of the work must deal with is Plath's portrayal of mental illness. On this issue, the reader has no trouble accepting the validity of Plath's presentation; both her descriptions of Esther's mental state and Plath's insights into the complexity of Esther's mind are truthful and compelling. Indeed, Plath's ability to be "real" on this level, on this issue, is perhaps the best key to the book's success.

However, this again creates a problem for the reader. The knowledge that Plath eventually killed herself affects our reading of the book. All our empathy and sympathy for Esther is tinged by the fact that we know that, eventually, Plath did not recover. We start to wonder what is wrong with Esther, and we also become angry with her for not surviving, but we are responding to an extra chapter – a final chapter that was never written, one that we are never allowed to read. Plath's real suicide, which we can never really fathom in poetic or fictional, or even analytic terms, affects our reading of Esther's attempted suicide.

So to come to terms with this complex situation we must talk about the mental illness of Sylvia/Esther. This is not an easy task, not even for a trained clinical psychologist.

However, leaving aside the question of whether Plath herself had a serious, constitutional and incurable mental problem (and I hate to use the word "illness" because even that word itself may not be quite accurate), and aside from whether or not Plath should be classified as schizophrenic or manic-depressive or merely neurotic, the critic, sensitive to the dilemma of the intelligent woman facing America in the fifties, can make several important observations.

First, Sylvia/Esther, or Esther/Sylvia, is obviously suffering from a lack of helpful supportive institutions and structures. There are no good support systems in her life, systems directed at the individual and the person that she is. Her mother does not understand her; her father is dead. The character of Mrs. Willard offers Esther only out-of-date platitudes. The character of Mrs. Guinea offers her a successful but slick and superficial view of life. The character of Jay Cee offers her professionalism, but at what cost? What young girl wants to become competent but emotionally sterile? In short, Esther/Sylvia has no attractive role models to follow. She does not want to learn shorthand and thereby follow her mother's role. She sees the inadequacies and hypocrisies of the other roles presented to her. This young girl has no idea *how to become herself*, and everyone is pressuring her to choose one of the inadequate role models. Esther would like to branch out in many directions, but she is told in subtle (and also in direct) ways that that route is not possible.

Besides the lack of support from an incomplete family (and certainly it is no one's fault that her father dies when Esther is nine years old), plus the lack of social support (it is too bad that Sylvia was not born twenty years later when the women's movement would have been supportive of her), Esther/Sylvia does not get much help from the professional world (Jay Cee doesn't really try to help her find a good job in New York City, nor do her college professors give her adequate guidance). In addition, Esther's treatment by her doctors and by her psychiatrists shows us how often the health professions fail people. The horror of imagining Esther being treated, first with insulin treatments and, then, electro-shock therapy is monstrous. The insensitivity of Esther's supposedly sensitive doctor who has promised her no electro-shock therapy without a discussion of it first is frightening. Esther's release from therapy before she has clearly defined herself and her problem points to poor medical practice. One reads in her journal that Plath, unable to sleep the last winter she lived in London, was prescribed sleeping pills by a British doctor. Considering her history, that seems quite irresponsible. Of course, the early 60s (Plath died in 1963) were times of a pill being a cure-all for everything.

All this makes us wonder if Plath, as well as her character Esther Greenwood, was not a victim of multiple failures created by the historical era that Plath was caught in. Concerning many matters, we can say only, "But if" or "If only." Yet those are the very *but*'s and *if*'s and *only*'s that we sigh whenever we view a tragedy.

Thus the attempted suicide of Esther and the real one of Sylvia Plath are another single tragedy for us to ponder. We see clearly that this tragedy is caused not only by a historical situation but also by old male-female conflicts, by a denial of death itself, and also probably by "the sickness of youth" – a condition well described by many German authors, some perhaps a bit akin to Sylvia Plath. It is impossible, one realizes finally, to analyze *The Bell Jar* without coming to terms with a host of modern existential dilemmas and without coming to terms with the problem of mental illness, or mental health, as it manifests itself in modern American society.

Esther Greenwood takes on several names and sees her friends as other parts of herself, or fragments of herself; indeed, she calls Joan Gilling her double – not just because Joan is having a nervous breakdown, but because Joan is a modern, dual-natured American. Esther, or perhaps even Sylvia, could not choose just one "fig," or one role – that is, she could not be just a mother, or "just a housewife," or just a one-dimensional editor, or a spinster professor; therefore, Esther had to invent other names and other masks. She could not accept the old traditional cliche that all these feelings and notions would leave her after she had a baby. Perhaps her several selves were actually a sign of mental *health*, for she did not repress her personality into one shape as so many others did. But society did not support her in this, and soon Esther is convinced that she is a hopeless mental case.

Being young and well educated does not help Esther much either. She knows enough to be bright and idealistic, has seen enough to be a bit cynical, and yet she has not had enough experience to temper this knowledge into wisdom. Worst of all, there are no survivors of the sort who can inspire her to struggle on. There are, unfortunately, no slightly batty, older, creative-type women around to tell her that there are lots of dangerous, interesting things one can try before deciding to commit suicide. Thus, Esther's idealism and cynicism only feed the "sour air" of her bell jar. They never lead to any truly outrageous acts or adventures. The loss of Esther's virginity is a dull, passionless event, safe within the confines of a math professor's apartment. One can only conclude that youth is certainly wasted on the young and that, yes, it is painful, but it is more a sickness of youth than a tragedy of youth because there is no Romeo and Juliet rashness of passion here. There is mostly just a loss of vision. Esther is no Joan of Arc. Nor in her sarcasm can she rise to the heights of a truly cynical youthful rebel. Even her "degeneracy" takes the form of just not bathing.

This lack of any howl of feeling, this barely trickling outlet of feeling is why Esther/Sylvia seems unable to come to terms with what her bell jar really means. Esther never truly affirms herself, and she never truly yields to herself either. She never says, "Here I am – take me or leave me" to anyone, and certainly never to herself. And she never accepts the ways in which she is like her mother, for example. (Of course, we must add, it is hard to affirm what one is when everyone is telling you to be something else. And why should a young rebellious girl yield to herself when she is so often forced to yield to other forces – the electro-shock therapy, for example.)

It is this superficiality in dealing with the underlying philosophical problems that actually feeds Esther's illness. And one of the major parts of this problem is not having control over her body, and not yet coming to terms with her body as a physical, animal entity which must be accepted. This is why the purchase of a diaphram is so important to Esther: it will allow her to be free of the *fear* of unwanted babies. But this simple purchase, fraught as it is with moral and social conflicts, does not ultimately solve or resolve the dilemma of how Esther feels about babies, nor how she feels about the purpose and destiny of her biological self. When she hemorrhages so badly from the loss of her virginity, we see that, indeed, the body is not always under one's control, and its functions and processes can easily extinguish one.

Perhaps it is this fear of the body that causes Esther to be so addicted to thoughts of suicide. For if the body is going to sabotage one, perhaps it would be best, easier to deal with, if one willfully killed the body first. Esther is thus afraid of life and afraid of death, afraid of success and afraid of failure. When these fears give her acute pain, the idea of death and joining her father in the grave seem to be the best solution.

Being so concerned with issues of freedom and entrapment (the bell jar is, after all, a kind of jail or even a kind of cocoon), Esther quite naturally attempts suicide when she cannot find any way out of her maze of fears and conflicts.

And here the critic must severely chastize the heroine for her lack of courage, her failure to even try very hard at being heroic. This book and its main character are so soaked in narcissism that even when this young girl fails, we are not sure how to react to that because the point of view of the work itself is not clear on some of these issues. In Kesey's *One Flew Over the Cuckoo's Nest*, the central character, McMurphy, fails to save himself, but he is nevertheless a hero, and we are quite clear about his individuality and where he stands in the battles he's undertaken. Esther keeps ducking her battles, and Plath never, in this work, crystalized what battle *might have been worth it* –

what 'figs' Esther might have tried to pick, or how many. So the book ends with a certain scattered quality, a certain flatness, a certain lack of finished thought. Release from the mental hospital is supposed to give Esther's character resolution, but actually, on reviewing the book as a whole, we see that Esther is probably still torn by fragmentation, and that she might even be lost again to depression.

What *The Bell Jar* gives us, finally, is a rather compelling story of a young girl who has, for a lack of a better way to say it, "a mental problem," a quite moving and probably very accurate account of mental health treatment in the 1950s. Beyond that, the author has failed us somewhat in not coming to terms with the underlying problems. The thinness of wisdom is regrettable. It is to be questioned again why Plath published the book under the name of Victoria Lucas. Did she finish it too quickly and could it have been made into a better book with more time? Would her next novel have been better; would it have had more depth? Perhaps later criticism can at least help put the book in different perspectives. The writer Tillie Olsen, in *Silences*, has said that this book is the only important novel that we have about the portrait of a young woman as an artist. In that light, perhaps the book deserves more credit.

And indeed, as it is, *The Bell Jar* is a wonderful document. But it, like so many of its characters, needs more dimension. Like Esther's 'figs,' we have just the several selves of Esther/Sylvia—Elly and Elaine. But where is the ethical dimension, where the courageous existential level? Where, finally, is the real, gritty self-questioning?

CHRONOLOGY OF PLATH

October 27, 1932	Sylvia Plath born to Aurelia Schober Plath, first generation American of Austrian descent, and Otto Emile Plath, emigré from Grabow in the Polish corridor. Otto Plath was a professor at Boston University; his specialty: entomology. Aurelia was approximately 20 years younger than her husband.
1935	Brother, Warren Joseph Plath, is born.
1937	The Plath family moves to Winthrop, Massachusetts.

1938	Sylvia begins public school at Winthrop and receives all A's; she is a model student.
November 5, 1940	Otto Plath dies of pneumonia and complications from diabetes.
1940-41	Aurelia Plath teaches secretarial studies at Boston University.
1942	Aurelia Plath moves her family, with her parents, to Wellesley.
1944	Sylvia enters Alice L. Phillips Junior High School.
1945	Plath's poem "The Spring Parade" published in the school's literary magazine.
1945-46	Other literary publications in *The Phillipian*, the school literary magazine.
1947	Plath wins Honorable Mention in The National Scholastic Literary contest. During these years her I.Q. tests in the 160s, and she meets a classmate, Richard Willard (a fictional name), who will continue with her in school. Later, she dates his older brother, "Buddy."
1950	Plath enters Smith College, Northampton, Massachusetts, on a scholarship. During this period, Buddy Willard asks her to the Yale prom.
1952	Plath wins the *Mademoiselle* fiction contest.
Summer, 1953	Plath is guest editor at *Mademoiselle*.
Late summer, 1953	Plath attempts suicide with sleeping pills. She is found and taken to Newton-Wellesley Hospital.

1953 (5 months)	Plath resides at McLean Hospital in Belmont, Massachusetts, and is treated with insulin and electro-shock therapy.
February, 1954	Plath returns to Smith.
1955	Plath graduates, goes to England on a Fulbright scholarship.
1956	Plath meets Ted Hughes in February. Marries him June 16 (Bloomsbury Day).
1956-57	Plath's second Cambridge year, English country trips.
1957-58	Returns to America with Hughes. Instructor in English, Smith College.
1958-59	Takes a hospital clerical job in Boston after quitting her Smith position to devote more time to writing. Plath also enrolls in Robert Lowell's poetry seminar and meets the poet Anne Sexton.
Fall, 1959	Plath writes at Yaddo, the writers retreat at Saratoga Springs, New York. In the winter, she and Ted return to England.
1960	Frieda Rebecca, born at home, April 1, London. November: *The Colossus* published in England.
1961	Plath suffers a miscarriage and has an appendectomy.
January 17, 1962	Nicholas Farrar born. *The Colossus* published in the United States.
September, 1962	Ted leaves Sylvia.

December, 1962	Plath moves to London, to a house once resided in by the poet William Butler Yeats.
January, 1963	*The Bell Jar*, published under the name Victoria Lucas, appears to generally favorable reviews.
February 11, 1963	Plath commits suicide in her London flat by turning on the gas jets.
1965	*Ariel* published in London.
1966	*Ariel* published in the United States.
1971	*The Bell Jar* published in the United States with Plath's name as author.
1981	*Collected Poems* published in the United States.
1982	*Journals* published in the United States.

INTRODUCTION TO THE NOVEL

Until the 1970s, American literature did not have a great many female heroines in its works of fiction, and too few of them had been created by women authors. We had Dreiser's Sister Carrie and Faulkner's and Sherwood Anderson's young girls and women; Hemingway left us the unforgettable Bret Ashley, but none of these characters came from the pens of women. Cather gave us Antonia, but this heroine seemed to be an idealized romantic 'other' of Cather herself. Flannery O'Connor, Eudora Welty, and Carson McCullers gave us memorable figures but who were they in relation to their authors? Perhaps the most personal, intimate insights to come from an American woman author had come from the poetry of Emily Dickinson and from Kate Chopin in her novel *The Awakening*, a piece relegated to obscurity until recently. But there were no women counterparts to Huck Finn; there were no women Gatsbys or Holden Caulfields, or Christopher Newmans.

There were, in short, no women writers creating women characters who spoke their minds; we had no parallels to Jane Austen's

Elizabeth; no American women were telling their readers what it is/was like to grow up in this vast and complex culture. If we are to understand the American female, using the idea that *women themselves* tell us what their lives are like and how they think and feel, we certainly need more fictional characters with more candor and insight and the courage to reveal themselves.

It is probably this vacuum in American literature that made *The Bell Jar's* protagonist so popular. Esther Greenwood: she is a college girl, a good student, a talented writer, and a fashion magazine contest winner; she is the well-bred oldest child in a typical family with two children, a clever games player, a semi-liberated budding intellectual, and a sexually confused late adolescent. Finally, she is a mental patient.

Esther lives in New England; she grows up in the 1930s and 40s, arrives in New York City just before her last year in college, and works on an apprenticeship for a fashion magazine. The year is 1953. This is before the popularity of the birth control pill, before women's liberation, and before all the major social movements of the 1960s. Esther Greenwood has achieved success in her academic endeavors and has won prizes for her writing. But her future and her female role are not clearly laid out for her. Indeed, how is she supposed to fuse her scholastic success with being a truly "feminine" creature of her era? That is a very real problem for Esther. She is plagued by her "fig-tree" metaphor/concept, in which each 'ripe fig' represents a different female role, and Esther cannot pick *just one*. As a result, she is afraid that they will all shrivel and drop off the tree before she can decide which one to choose.

Esther reaches maturity in the early 1950s in an America where women's roles were rigidly assigned. Basically, American women fell into two groups: the good girls and the bad girls. Good girls married well and had 2.5 children, possibly more but not too many more. They kept nice houses, cooked proper, nutritious, and economical meals, went to PTA meetings, and in general, they were dutiful "wives." If they were successful in life, they became very much like Mrs. Eisenhower, or Mrs. Nixon, or Doris Day. The bad girls, in contrast, were sexy, bosomy, probably blonde, and they did *not* marry proper lawyers and doctors and politicians. They might, if they were clever, become lesser Marilyn Monroe types. Then there were also a group of women who were not really considered women. These were the spinsters and librarians and social workers and old maid school teachers. These intelligent women, these Ethel Rosenbergs, (cited by Esther in the first paragraph of the novel), were doomed in society. They were not classified as good or bad because they did not "play the game" for male attention.

Thus, the good girls and the bad girls were classified and identified in terms of their relationship to men and society; they were *not* given value in terms of their own personalities, talents, and endeavors. Esther Greenwood is terribly aware of this problem of being shoved by society into an "either/or" situation. This dilemma is portrayed in New York City through the characters of Doreen (the 'bad' girl) and Betsy (the 'good' girl). The one startling characteristic that Esther has is that she *intends* to defy any role or life path that will pigeonhole her into being one kind of woman or another. Esther Greenwood wants to be herself, and to be an individual. She wants her American birthright. This is why she keeps saying over and over, "I Am I Am I Am."

But this task she has set for herself is overwhelming. How can she integrate the good girl, the 'A' student, with the fashion-conscious, man-teasing young lady? How can she integrate the innocent, pure young woman who loves cleanliness with the young woman who has intense sexual desires? How can she integrate the person who wants to be a poet with the person who wants to be a mother? How can she integrate the young woman who wants to travel and have many lovers with the one who wants to be a wife? And as Esther proceeds, at a rapid pace, first through her terms at college, then on to New York City, the center of the sophisticated chic world, she becomes more and more frightened that she will not be able to pick only one role, one 'fig.' This is tragic because there are no successful, interesting whole women to encourage Esther to pick all the 'figs' she can. Indeed, Esther is constantly being warned and restricted by the adult women of her world. "Watch out, Esther," they all seem to say, and perhaps with some cause. Then Ethel Rosenberg is electrocuted. There is clearly not much encouragement for women to be individual, to be different, and to be brave and daring.

So Esther, confused and scared, heroically struggles on, keeps up her grades, tries to be fashionable, and she begins to play games. She develops other names for herself, as if that will solve the problems of multiple roles and a fractured identity. She lies to her teachers, her editor, her mother, and to her friends – usually in situations where it is not useful to her, or to the advancement of her career. She lies mostly to play games and to protect herself from conflict. She is deathly afraid of revealing her true identity, or her muddled identity, to anyone. And she is certainly not ready to fight others for it. Because of these fears and conflicts, Esther has no really close friends. None of her friends truly know her, and even if it is true that her mother and her editor and her teachers cannot understand her, Esther certainly doesn't allow them to try.

Esther is desperately in need of help to get herself from adolescence into adulthood; she continually cuts herself off from others and from her own feelings, as well. She is convinced that her father might have helped her, but, she sighs, he died long ago. Thus, she feels all alone and Esther's world becomes grayer and grayer as she becomes more and more in conflict with herself and depressed about herself. After her stint in New York City, she has a severe mental breakdown and, eventually, she takes sleeping pills in an almost fatal suicide attempt.

When Esther is institutionalized and treated, she is, of course, not in charge of her own life at all. She feels that she is in a bell jar, stewing in her own foul air. Meanwhile, her mother, and Mrs. Guinea, and even Buddy and some of her girl friends, plus the institutions for mental health and the proverbial wheels of American good will – all these are trying to piece Esther back together again, in their image of what she was or *should be*. No wonder we are so sympathetic with this bright, sometimes charming, attractive, but victimized young woman.

One of the major causes for Esther's breakdown – that is, the lack of a clear individualized female role – is not dealt with at all in her treatment. How can Esther get well when she is subjected to the same forces and pressures that made her ill in the first place? Dr. Nolan is a kind and helpful woman, but, for the most part, she treats Esther's *symptoms* – not her problem.

As the reader follows Esther through all her trials and misfortunes, we begin to see a young American girl whom we never knew existed. We see how she feels, how she is bad, how she is good, how she is dumb, and how she is smart. Most of all, we see how human she is, and we want her to make it – to survive. But after Esther's recovery from her breakdown and as she prepares to leave the "asylum," after

Joan's (her double's) suicide, we feel apprehensive about her future. We wish desperately that Esther would tell them all to mind their own business, that she's going to do it her way. But she does not seem to have that strength of Huckleberry Finn. And again the reader is brought back to Sylvia Plath, Esther's creator, and we mourn for the victimization of one of our first, authentic young American female voices. If Esther is the darker side of Plath, a voice from her more negative side, we are indeed sorry Plath did not live long enough to give us another female character – perhaps a more mature and bright, and certainly a more positive woman.

LIST OF CHARACTERS

Esther Greenwood

The "I" of *The Bell Jar*.

Buddy Willard

Esther's boyfriend, the son of one of her mother's friends. Buddy is a student at Yale; he plans to be a doctor.

Doreen

The glamorous, sexy, fiction contest winner from the South. She and Esther meet in New York City, where Doreen tries to help Esther with clothes and men.

Jay Cee

Editor of *Ladies' Day* magazine; she is Esther's boss in New York City. Jay Cee is a somewhat dowdy, but a competent professional woman.

Betsy

The *Ladies' Day* winner from the Midwest. Bright and ingenuous, Betsy becomes a model. As Esther's "innocent" friend, Betsy lends her a skirt and blouse for Esther's trip home.

Gladys

Waitress on the Cape. Buddy Willard has an affair with her.

Lenny Shepherd

New York disc jockey who dresses like a cowboy. He seduces Doreen.

Frankie

Friend of Lenny.

Elly Higginbottom

Esther's New York pseudonym, used at such times as her excursion to Lenny's, when she wishes to be incognito.

Esther's Grandfather

He works at a country club and introduces Esther to caviar and vichyssoise. He jokes that he will supply all the caviar she can eat for Esther's wedding.

Hilda

A tall, green-eyed girl, one of the fashion contest winners; she makes startling hats.

Esther's Mother

Mrs. Greenwood teaches shorthand and typing to support the family after Esther's father dies.

Mr. Manzi

Teaches physics and chemistry at Esther's college.

Philomena Guinea

Esther's patroness, a wealthy novelist whose first book is made into a silent film starring Bette Davis.

Constantin

A simultaneous interpreter for the UN. Mrs. Willard gives him Esther's phone number.

Socrates and Attila

Men with interesting names that Esther has "collected."

Mrs. Willard

Buddy's mother. She has a college degree but spends most of her time housekeeping. She has many theories on relationships between men and women.

Joan Gilling

A sporting girl from Esther's hometown who has dated Buddy. She hangs herself after a brief period in a mental hospital.

Will

A third-year medical student who thinks that Esther shouldn't watch a baby being born.

Jody

Esther's best (and only) girl friend in college.

Eric

A boy whom Esther comforts when his girl friend jilts him. She thinks she'd like to go to bed with him.

Mr. Willard

Buddy's father. A shy economics professor, married to Mrs. Willard. He takes Esther to the Adirondacks to visit Buddy.

Marco

A Peruvian who assaults Esther on their first date.

Mrs. Ockenden

A neighbor of the Greenwoods. She reports Esther's behavior to Mrs. Greenwood.

Dodo Conway

A neighbor of the Greenwoods; she has six children and is pregnant again.

Elaine

The heroine in Esther's "novel."

Dr. Gordon

The psychiatrist who is recommended to Esther.

George Bakewell

A remote acquaintance of Esther; he visits her in the mental hospital where he is the houseman.

Mrs. Mole

A red-haired patient at hospital who has to be locked up for her erratic behavior.

Dr. Nolan

Esther's female psychiatrist at the hospital.

Valerie & Miss Norris

Patients at the mental hospital.

DeeDee & Loubelle

Other patients at the mental hospital.

Mrs. Savage

A patient in the hospital; a former Vassar girl.

Miss Huey

The nurse who administers electro-shock therapy.

Milly & Theodora

Girls at Esther's college who are thought to be lesbians.

Dr. Quinn

Joan's psychiatrist, a single lady.

Nurse Kennedy

A woman whom Joan shares an apartment with when she is an out-patient, where Esther goes after her date with Irwin.

Irwin

A young mathematician and college professor; Esther very rationally "chooses" him to make love to her for the first time.

CRITICAL COMMENTARIES

CHAPTERS 1-4

The first sentence of Sylvia Plath's *The Bell Jar* alerts the reader to the conflicts that will be dealt with in this semi-autobiographical novel: "It was a queer, sultry summer, the summer they electrocuted the Rosenbergs, and I didn't know what I was doing in New York." The speaker will tell us in the next few sentences that she is "stupid" and that she feels "sick," and that she is preoccupied with death. Like Holden Caulfield in *Catcher in the Rye*, this young, college age, girl-woman is experiencing an adolescent crisis.

Summer is usually thought of as being a happy, fun time for students. It is a time of vacation from studies, a time to travel and relax, have fun with friends. Sometimes students work, but even that is a short-term commitment, and thus more relaxed. The speaker of *The Bell Jar* has gone to New York City for a month, and she will relate her varied "fun" experiences to us, but she is not happy. She works, too, but not with any pleasure. Indeed, she is confused and is in conflict with all aspects of her life.

When Esther Greenwood tells us in the first sentence that this is "the summer they electrocuted the Rosenbergs," we get a picture not only of that summer's being nauseating, sultry and death-oriented, but that this young girl's attitudes and life experiences are also this way. She is not a happy, carefree coed off for a summer fling, even if it appears that way. She is about to have a major nervous breakdown.

Esther Greenwood is steeped in the "mirage-gray at the bottom of their granite canyons"; her New York world is filled with images of cadavers. For example, she says, "I knew something was wrong with me that summer" and then proceeds to tell us about how she skips the social events which she is supposed to attend, how she is called into her editor's office, and how she and her friends get violently sick from tainted food. In between her account of her job, which she "won" through a fashion magazine contest, she recounts her past and her recent college experiences. She goes into detail about her reactions to her chemistry classes, which she calls "death," and how she schemed so that she did not have to take chemistry for credit. She also tells us that her boyfriend, Buddy Willard, a pre-med student, showed her a cadaver.

She also gives us glimpses of her future; we hear, for instance that "last week I cut the plastic starfish off the sunglasses case for the baby to play with." (The case was one of the free gifts that Esther "won" with her job.) So we realize, even in Chapter 1, that Esther, the bright, clever, all-American successful girl, so immersed in death and despair, does survive her college years to go on to a life that includes a baby.

The task given to the reader is to try to figure out why Esther is so filled with conflict, so alienated. She herself says, "I was supposed to be having the time of my life." So why is she so miserable with her success? Why does she feel the need to invent another name for herself, "Elly Higginbottom"? Why does she try to be pals with Doreen? (Doreen is a glamor girl much like the wealthy Katy Gibbs girls who live at the Amazon hotel where Esther is staying.) Why does Esther avoid her magazine work if she really does like her boss, Jay Cee? Does Esther really want to be a writer? What does Esther want from life? How does she really feel about herself and her world? Does she perceive reality correctly? What kind of change is she going through?

The reader should pay close attention to the images that Esther gives us of New York; they clearly reveal that something is wrong. When Doreen and Esther find themselves in a cab in a traffic jam, they allow themselves to be picked up by a man (Lenny) in a blue lumber shirt and his short runty friend; we feel sure that other things are probably going to go wrong too. At Lenny's place, Esther starts to feel increasingly withdrawn and unattractive. Sexy Doreen is having a great time, so Esther leaves by half-sliding down a banister, and then she decides to walk back to the Amazon Hotel by following her street map. In her room, she is depressed by the silence and her bedside telephone which does not ring. She takes a long "dissolving" bath and goes to bed. When the night maid helps the drunk Doreen to her door, Esther decides that it's best to leave her on the carpet. Doreen vomits, and Esther vows to be loyal to "Betsy and her innocent friends." In the morning Doreen is gone, and the hall is empty.

If Doreen is the slinky, glamorous southern girl, whose college is very fashion conscious (the girls have pocketbook covers made to match all their dresses), Betsy is the import from Kansas who innocently tells a producer about male and female corn. Ironically, it is Betsy who has her hair cut and is made into a cover girl. She and Doreen appear headed for different kinds of success, one coming from innocence and work, the other from using her beauty to trap men, like Lenny, the disc jockey with the white bearskin rug and the apartment filled with Indian rugs. Esther/Elly represents the New England "Yankee" girl, one with extraordinary perceptions. She is also the only girl of the lot who does not seem able to fit into a glamorous role. The other girls fit some "image," but Esther, because of the insights which she is sharing with the reader, slips in and out of an ugly duckling state. She tells us she is five-foot-ten, but we never see her as a tall, attractive or sensitive contest winner because she seems to feel she is deficient—when compared to Doreen and Betsy.

Esther says that she likes "looking on at other people in crucial situations." Is she creating a crucial situation, in part, for herself so she can examine it? Or is it that since she has been "studying and reading and writing and working like mad" all her life, she doesn't know how to accept a sociable, much less a fashionable role? The successful Jay Cee tries to encourage Esther to follow her as a role model, because the homely but competent editor knows all the "quality writers"; she tells Esther to "learn French and German and probably several other languages." This reminds Esther of her dilemma with physics and chemistry and after that story, the reader wonders if Esther really does "love school." Perhaps she secretly wants to be sexy like Doreen – or perhaps naively innocent like Betsy.

At the *Ladies' Day* banquet, Esther *gorges* on caviar and chicken slices, avocado and crabmeat salad. We realize here that she *does not* have "perfect manners" because she tells about the time when she drank from the fingerbowl at her patron's, Mrs. Guinea's, luncheon. Here, where she gorges on caviar, she does so because her grandfather, who works for a country club, has introduced her to caviar and has given her a taste for expensive things. But if Esther seems to think that she knows how to please herself at free banquets, she does not know how to navigate the other areas of high life in New York. And when she becomes almost deathly ill from food poisoning, she does not understand what has happened. We feel full of anxiety about her ambivalence and conflicts, and we wonder if it is the food or her insights which cause Esther to be sick. Since she and Betsy become ill at a Technicolor, football-romance movie, the reader suspects that their illness might be caused by an over-indulgence in *not only* crabmeat, but in New York life itself.

Thus, Chapter 4 ends with Esther's surviving a serious sickness from which she feels a certain purification. And there are some positive aspects. Esther receives many presents from the magazine, and her appetite returns as soon as Doreen visits her. "I'm starving," Esther says. Indeed, Esther is starved, but she is starved for more than just food. She lacks love, good parental guidance, affection, a meaningful friendship, and a clear sense of direction for her life. At times, she spitefully blames others for her unhappiness or points to the inadequacies and hypocrisies of the 1950s. At other times, Esther, like a Dostoevskian character, blames her own dark, perverse tendencies. She is also, it seems, starved for answers. She does not know *why* she feels the way she does, and at times, she does not really know *how* she feels. Basically, Esther is at war with herself; nature pulls her one way, and her social training pulls her another, and her unusual and perceptive insights pull her yet another way. The New York world of whirlwind fashion events and professional engagements is clearly a shock, especially for a studious girl who arrives fresh from her sheltered New England existence. No wonder Esther so easily succumbs to the poisoned city crabmeat.

Our central image of Esther, at this point, is of a starved girl. She is starved physically because of the results of food poisoning, but, more important, she has been starved psychologically from the beginning of the book. On one hand, she takes in everything about the city, all its myriad images, all its smells, sounds, and sights. But none of this nourishes her. The subway's mouth is "fusty, peanut-smelling"; the "goggle-eyed headlines" stare at her; and the "granite canyons" are "mirage-gray." Esther feels as if she is carrying around a cadaver's head. She concludes that something is wrong with *her*, but the reader also wonders if there is not something wrong with Esther's world. Is not the city, with all its clamor and excitement, its pollutions and stimulations, a major part of Esther's problem? Esther cannot take all this in, cannot find nourishment and refreshment, so her mind's reaction is to look harder, to try to take in more, to strain to examine all of the new images and evidence. But Esther is constantly led back to death. The city means death to her, a high-tension death like the electrocution of the Rosenbergs. Finally, even Esther's body is poisoned by the city, and she becomes thoroughly sick. In her attempt to recover, she becomes ravenous for chicken soup and other nourishment.

It is at this point, because of her unhappiness with New York, that Esther starts to relate her memories about her romance with Buddy, as well as some of her childhood and college memories, as if to try to figure out how she got to this gray world of *Ladies' Day* magazine, in a summer that was supposed to be a high point in her life.

One of the keys to these first chapters, to Esther's character, and perhaps even to her mental problems is the fashion theme. Fashion is everything – how a person "looks" is extremely important. Certainly the girls who work for the magazine are programmed into the newest colors and styles. They are to be *the* example for millions of college girls. They are to dress correctly and be photographed as "endorsing" that "certain look" to all the young, wealthy "in" college girls.

Being in fashion and looking good, dressing correctly, and stylishly are synonymous with success. This is the year that black patent leather is in style. Is it no wonder that even the fashion fun of New York City cannot make Esther forget the Rosenbergs and her own thoughts of death?

Thus, Esther starts to wear more black, more than just her black shoes and black purse. She dresses in a black shantung sheath dress for fancy occasions. In contrast, Doreen, who is smart and cynical, and whose comments at *Ladies' Day* functions keep Esther from being bored, wears white and lots of frothy silk lingerie. Yet even Doreen's white lace dress does not make her look innocent and pure. Esther sees Doreen as "dusky as a bleached-blonde Negress." Betsy, on the other hand, Esther's other friend on the magazine staff, the girl who is called Pollyanna Cowgirl by Doreen, is quite genuinely innocent in her Midwestern ways. She is not sophisticated enough, as the southern Doreen and the New England Esther, to really understand what is happening that summer, but the magazine's beauty editor makes a cover girl out of Betsy, and Betsy keeps on smiling her "Sweetheart of Sigma Chi smile."

Esther vacillates between wanting to be cynical like Doreen and innocent like Betsy. In some ways, Esther is like both girls, and this shows us how divided she is. It is perhaps this tendency toward a split personality that gives Esther part of her mental problems.

In addition, Esther keeps lying about things. She lies about who she is; she calls herself Elly Higgenbottom. We ask ourselves: why does Esther allow herself to be in situations where she does not even want to admit her true identity? She seems to *want* these fast life experiences, such as going to the disc jockey's apartment, but she doesn't want anyone to know about it, especially these apparently contemptible New Yorkers. She worries about her manners and how she appears, yet at the *Ladies' Day* luncheon she kids herself that her gluttony in eating all the caviar is all right – and has to remind herself of the poet whom she met who ate his salad with his fingers and was so poised at it that it seemed the right thing to do.

Esther is plagued by the idea of doing the *right* thing, but she constantly wants to act otherwise. When Jay Cee calls her and tries to advise her and give her some help, however limited, Esther's response is that Jay Cee said terrible things to her. Her guilt about following the right forms even impedes her judgment. And then she has to confess and tell us how she got her chemistry credit in college from poor Mr. Manzi by fraudulent means. Finally, she and Betsy end up vomiting in the back of a taxicab, after the luncheon and the movie. This is certainly a horrible way for a fashion-conscious young girl, guilt-ridden by social manners, to behave.

Yet only two chapters earlier, when she escaped from an almost equally terrible scene in Lenny's apartment, she found her own silence depressing—just as she does now. It is Esther's inability to communicate—even with herself—that leads to these terrible scenes. And when Doreen gets drunk and lies sick outside her door, Esther just leaves her there. She is not even able to help her friend. She is seemingly devoid of human caring. But then, we cannot expect starving people, weak as they are, to be able to summon up human kindness and help others. Often, such people cannot even help themselves.

CHAPTERS 5-8

The day after Esther's food poisoning experience, she is too sick to go to work, and she is resting when she receives a phone call from a man. He turns out to be Constantin, a simultaneous interpreter from the UN whom Mrs. Willard knows. Esther is excited—partly because she likes to "collect" men with unusual names. Then she is disappointed when she realizes that he is calling her as a favor to Mrs. Willard. But she does accept his invitation to visit the UN and then have a "bite to eat." Constantin's choosing of words, via Mrs. Willard, immediately causes Esther to be annoyed with him. His call reminds her of Buddy Willard's hypocrisy that she so despises. It also reminds her of all the minor problems with social manners that she finds so disconcerting—such as, how much to tip. Esther seems to have a difficult time negotiating simple things such as breakfast in bed. So she decides to read; she reads a story about a fig tree, a Jewish man, and a nun. This again makes her think of Buddy, and how he once told her that a poem is "just a piece of dust." She could not think of a smart reply until now—a year later.

For the next chapter and a half, we learn about Esther's recent relationship with Buddy and how she adored him from a distance for several years. Their mothers were good friends, and their fathers were both university professors. When Buddy visits her at college, she is elated until she finds out that he is there to have a date with Joan. She becomes sarcastic with him, and Buddy leaves somewhat crestfallen. When Esther opens the envelope that Buddy leaves with her, her mood turns to joy when she discovers that he has asked *her* to the Yale Junior Prom. What a coup for the bookworm Esther.

Again, Esther's big date with Buddy is a mixed experience. She describes Buddy as being rather cheap, and her accommodations for the prom weekend are rather meager. For the high-point of the date, Buddy takes Esther up the hill behind the chemistry lab. She admits that the view is beautiful, but she is not exactly in awe of it. When Buddy kisses her, Esther is not as enthusiastic as he is, but she says nothing to him. He proposes to see her every third weekend, and Esther, at this suggestion, is "almost fainting and dying to get back to college and tell everybody." We then learn that she apparently continues to see Buddy steadily, even after he goes to medical school, despite her lack of interest in his kisses. The irony then is that she says it took her a long time to find out what a *hypocrite* he was, when, in fact, she found out about his hypocrisy very early. Yet Esther too is somewhat of a hypocrite. She is not even romantically interested in Buddy, but leads him to believe that she is.

As Buddy is portrayed by Esther, the reader does not envision him as a dashing suitor. But what one cannot fathom is why Esther spent so much time with him, and so much time recounting a relationship with a boy whom she obviously did not like very much. Furthermore, she does not even seem to realize that Buddy does actually rather like her more than she likes him. Later, Buddy proudly shows her a poem of his that has been published – probably to please her, even if he does say that a poem is "just a piece of dust." Seemingly, Buddy is trying to compete with Esther in her field; but since he has no ambition to be a poet, we sense that in a simple-minded way, he is trying to draw closer to her.

Buddy takes Esther to see a baby being born, and we realize that he has attempted to involve her in his field before, with lectures on sickle-cell anemia and other "depressing diseases." He also shows her cadavers and babies preserved in bottles. We recall Esther's aversion to chemistry and physics, and we see clearly that Buddy and Esther are quite mismatched, as far as interests go. He tells Esther that there must be something in poetry if a girl like her is interested in it, and she tries to explain poems to him, but his mind does not seem to focus on the subject. After one such session, he responds by asking her if she's ever "seen a man," and he proceeds to undress in front of her. Buddy is always the clinical med student; Esther is always the sensitive, ambivalent poet. Buddy is practical and conventional; Esther is philosophical and unconventional. However, sometimes Esther has practical insights that go against the grain. For example, when she watches the birth of the baby and Buddy explains that the woman is under the influence of twilight sleep and that she won't remember a thing afterwards, Esther notes that the woman is moaning from the pain, and Esther thinks one might as well be awake and see the baby born if one is going to have the pain anyway.

Esther is also direct (and practical) with Buddy when she asks him if he's ever had an affair. He tells her the story of his affair with Gladys, the waitress, and Esther is quite shocked at how many times Buddy slept with the waitress during the summer when he was a busboy on the Cape. Because Esther knows so little about sex, or about relationships between men and women, she asks the other girls at school about this "other woman." They all respond that "men are like that," and they imply that Esther should "just accept it." Esther can't stand the double standard of the world, and she is angry because Buddy treats her as if she is so sexy and then acts so pure himself. Significantly, Esther recounts all this to the reader before she goes out on a date with Constantin. Remember that one of her motivations for dating him is to try to have sex with someone so that she and Buddy "will be even." Yet on the other hand, after Buddy goes to the Adirondacks for the tuberculosis cure, Esther uses him as an excuse to stay in her room and study. So we see that her behavior during her summer in New York is somewhat different from her previous semester in college. Now, she seems to feel a need to grow up – to have an affair – as well as try to come to grips with the "real" professional world of the city.

On her date with Constantin, Esther again has mixed feelings. She thinks that he's too short, but still "sort of handsome." She also says that he has intuition, a quality which she thinks that most American men lack. He drives her away in a green convertible, and she feels happier than when she was nine and ran with her father on the beach. It is now (Chapter 7) that we learn that Esther thinks that she was only happy until she was nine years old. She's had all kinds of lessons since then – dance, art, and music – and she's been to college, but she's never been happy, apparently, since her father died.

In addition to her thoughts of unhappiness, versus her earlier bliss, Esther starts to think of all her deficiencies. She can't cook, can't take shorthand (her mother's specialty), can't ski, or ride a horse (because they cost too much, she says). She is only good at winning scholastic and literary prizes, and she fears that these opportunities may be coming to an end. Then comes her image of the fig tree. She sees one fig (rather than a branch) as a husband, family, and children; another fig as a poet, then one as a brilliant professor, one as "Ee Gee" – a parallel to Jay Cee – one as a traveler, one as a "pack of lovers," one as an Olympic lady crew champion, and she sees many, many more figs. But Esther feels that she can – and must – choose *only one* fig, and she can't make up her mind which one she wants. She wants to "shoot off in all directions" and doesn't believe that is possible. Buddy, of course, has told her that after she has a baby she won't care about being a poet any more. Esther can't accept that idea. She wants all the figs, and she fears that they will wither and fall off the tree before she has made up her mind which one to pick.

When she goes to dinner with Constantin, Esther fails to realize her very real dilemma. She says that maybe she was just hungry – that's why she was thinking of the fig tree. She is unable to push forward with her vision of a diverse and interesting life for herself. Instead, she eats hungrily and decides to let Constantin seduce her. After listening to music sitting on his balcony, Esther retires to the bedroom. When she awakens, she again wonders if she's been poisoned. But no, she is physically fine, and except for her thoughts on marriage as a slave state, she is quite well. Constantin combs her hair with his fingers, which gives her an electric-like shock, but she returns to her hotel still a virgin.

At the hotel, an old leg-break injury starts to ache; the old injury throbs and reminds her of her pains from the past, pains that still seem to impede her life. She's again reminded of Buddy, the thorn in her side, and how she broke her leg skiing with him. Chapter 8 is a recall of her visit to Buddy's sanatorium, how Mr. Willard took her there and told her on the trip that he and Mrs. Willard always wanted a daughter like her. She feels dull and disappointed on this gray trip, partly because it was the day after Christmas; when she sees Buddy's liver-colored habitation, she is even more depressed. In addition, Buddy has become fat. And in this terrible setting, he asks her to marry him. No wonder she thinks American men have no intuition. Buddy is certainly a klutz. But then, the reader can see that both Buddy and Esther are very adolescent and very inexperienced. She responds by telling Buddy that she'll never marry.

They go skiing, and Buddy tries to help her, even though Esther thinks that what he suggests is foolhardy. But, having suicidal thoughts, she decides to try to go down a big hill even though she doesn't know how to zig-zag. She seems easily influenced to self-destructiveness. Thus she flies to the bottom of the hill and is "doing fine until the man stepped into her path." She breaks her leg in two places and believes that Buddy is really quite happy about it. Throughout the story, Esther is "doing fine" until something or someone—a man usually—steps in her path. Then things go awry, and she always ends up as a crumpled mess. In college, the chemistry class stepped in her path, and in New York City, violent sex stepped into the crowded streets in the guise of Lenny. Later, when Esther goes home, we discover that the letter of non-acceptance for the *male* instructor's writing course had arrived; this letter ruins Esther's summer plans. We recall, then, when Esther was nine: her father died unexpectedly, ruining her idyllic life. Esther seems bent on rushing towards her projected goals, and she doesn't know what to do when the plans are changed, especially when they are changed by a force outside herself, usually a man.

Esther's trip to the Adirondacks not only ends with a broken leg; it is another gray experience that reminds her that "promises never come to pass." It makes her think that perhaps she should become a Catholic—an idea that comes to her whenever she is in a tight spot or depressed. She fantasizes that being a Catholic would solve all her problems—if she became a really devout Catholic.

It must be noted here that it is not that Esther's experiences are so unusual, but that it is her *perception* of them that is so different. Millions of American girls have had mixed feelings about their virginity, about whether or not to swallow their distaste and marry a soon-to-be successful but egotistical and dull student. Even more college-age girls have had skiing accidents, probably. And many have gone off to New York City, or other cities, or exotic places to try to find their fortune and their adulthood. What makes *The Bell Jar* a compelling book, besides its being a truthful, if superficial, rendering of this adolescent dilemma, is that Esther Greenwood is experiencing this in 1953. Esther is obviously years ahead of the women's liberation movement of the 1970s. What makes Esther so appealing is that she is so alone. And, of course, it is her extreme alienation that leads to her suicide attempt.

One of the major themes of these four chapters is that, for Esther, life is mostly like the day after Christmas, a day when she usually feels "overstuffed and dull and disappointed." The promises of Esther's young life too often turn out to be unsatisfying. She has adored Buddy from afar, yet his kisses do not affect her when he finally shows an interest in her. In short, Esther does not seem able to find a relationship with honesty in it, and she cannot even enjoy dating in a superficial way. Yet she is driven to want to date men – perhaps mostly because of social convention, but also because she is embarrassed to study in her room on Saturday nights. When Buddy is in the TB hospital, that relieves her of an obligation to date. For a brief time, she is happy not to be bothered with social plottings.

But, if on one hand she is driven to date, Esther can't stand Buddy for his hypocrisy. Yet she needs him. This, in turn, makes her as much a hypocrite as Buddy. Esther is dishonest with Buddy about her responses to the hospital situations, and she can't even tell him her reaction to his naked body.

Esther's training in social manners contributes to her being trapped. She is rebelling from an excessive emphasis on "be nice, be nice." Thus, she mocks people even when it is not necessary. Esther is too acutely aware of manners and styles. For example, when Constantin asks her for a "bite to eat," she knows, and hates, that phrase because it belongs to Mrs. Willard. If Constantin has "intuition," as Esther thinks he has, perhaps that is why he doesn't seduce her, because in spite of the "electric shock" he gives her, she is mainly interested in "getting even" with Buddy for his "infidelities."

Torn between the "should's" of her New England upbringing and the pressures of her peers to have men in her life, Esther cannot reconcile her feelings about men – much less have warm relationships with them. She has no way to deal with her negative thoughts, which her social training tells her are, if not wrong, at least unattractive. But if Esther cannot avoid men, or be successful just using them, at least she could give them a piece of her mind occasionally. Yet she never even writes to Buddy to tell him about her insights on his poem, his "piece of dust." Surely, even for Esther, that would have been permissible. But she keeps all this inside herself, and then it comes out in peculiar ways, mostly harmful to Esther herself.

Esther says that she is not practical. But does she try to be? Why not look for a boyfriend who is suitable? Does Esther, indeed, ever ask herself what kind of man would be best for her? She has not learned to do any of the choosing. Instead, she is always too concerned about how men look. And, with her sharp scrutiny, she always finds something wrong – Constantin, for example, is too short; Buddy becomes repulsively fat when he is ill. Clearly, Esther is very dissatisfied with *herself*. She makes lists of all the things she can't do. Her disappointments always lead her back to her shattered visions. She decides that if she expects nothing, she will not be disappointed. Is it to be all or nothing for her? Thinking that the era of winning prizes is over for her, Esther can do nothing except focus on her social (real and imagined) failures. She is easily embarrassed. She has a "sickness of the will," because when she sees any small defect in herself, she sees it as being something monumentally wrong with her. She can be witty and clever, and insightful about her situation, but she cannot respond with real laughter or wisdom. Thus she is being driven more and more, by society and her own character and actions, into alienation, into real, physical sickness. She is letting her trivial disappointments poison her, and she is becoming duller and duller because she cannot choose, cannot say *no*, and cannot speak out. She is overstuffed on her successes and her dreams, and she needs the purgative of reality and humor. Instead, she will be assaulted with more of New York City and the cruel summer of 1953.

CHAPTERS 9 & 10

The sensitive side of Esther is aghast that Hilda, the girl who is extremely fashion conscious, is wearing lots of "bile green"; even this latest fashion color seems to say, "I'm glad they're going to die" – meaning the Rosenbergs. Esther's response to the Rosenbergs' electrocution is quite different from many of the girls' opinions, but she never voices her opinions or argues with others about their conservative or cruel opinions. As with Buddy's comment on his poem being only dust, we see that it has taken Esther years to get the courage to even consider presenting her negative views about her associates.

At the end of the *Ladies' Day* sojourn, all the girls are to have their pictures taken with something that symbolizes their future. Betsy is having her picture taken with corn to represent her plans to marry a farmer. No one can decide what might best represent Esther's desire to be a poet. Then Jay Cee cuts a rose off her hat, and Esther is posed for her picture; but before it can be taken, she bursts into tears and is left weeping on the pink loveseat in her editor's office.

For the finale of Esther's New York stay, Doreen has arranged a blind date for Esther with an attractive Peruvian. Before the date, Esther is plagued with indecision, especially about her clothes, so Doreen wraps Esther's clothes in a ball and throws them under the bed. The date, a rich suburban dance affair, is a young girl's classic horror date. The suave Marco gives Esther his diamond stickpin at the beginning of the date in a grand romantic gesture. Then he proceeds to order the evening for his liking. So Esther drinks daiquiris, and even though she protests that she really doesn't know how to dance, Marco forcefully sweeps her to the dance floor telling her to "pretend you are drowning." Now she learns why many women love men who are womenhaters, she tells us – from a distance, of course – for this is Esther the adult narrator speaking. The mesmerizing Marco leads Esther outside, where he throws her to the ground and rips her dress down to the waist. She kicks and hits him until he is at bay, and when he demands his stickpin back, she leaves him searching for it in her small bag in the mud. Back at her hotel, she goes onto the roof and throws her newly acquired, expensive clothes off the parapet, one by one, piece by piece. She describes these gray scraps as being like "a loved one's ashes."

On the train home, wearing Betsy's skirt and blouse that she acquired by trading her bathrobe for them, Esther sees herself as a sick Indian with pieces of dried blood on her face. Now, as Esther is becoming more and more depressed, more and more of her life is described as gray. Her suitcase, for example, is gray, filled with two dozen unripe avocados that Doreen has, quite lovingly it seems, given Esther as a farewell present. And when Esther arrives home, she crawls into her mother's *gray* Chevrolet. This will be Esther's first summer in the suburbs because she failed to get into the writing course she wanted so desperately to be accepted for. She says, "I had nothing to look forward to." The situation seems even bleaker when Esther awakens on her first morning home; it is unclear which of the Greenwood neighbors irritates Esther more – the busybody Mrs. Ockenden who spies on Esther when Mrs. Greenwood is at work, or "the breeder," Dodo Conway, who has six children and is expecting another, "Catholic that she is." "Children make me sick," says Esther.

When Esther's friend Jody calls from Cambridge about the room they might share for summer school, Esther knows that it is wrong to decline, but she is unable to call Jody back and, thus, Esther is stuck in the suburbs – stuck in an atmosphere that is as hateful as New York City was confusing. In her indecision about how to spend the summer, Esther vacillates – thinking that she will write a novel about a girl called Elaine, then deciding to learn shorthand from her mother in the evenings, then deciding to read *Finnegan's Wake* by James Joyce, and then writing her honors thesis. But, plan after plan is discarded. Esther's mother tries to reason sweetly with her, but to no avail. The shorthand lessons only give Esther a headache. She decides that she can't write a novel because she doesn't have enough experience in life yet. She wonders if her college career would have been more successful if she had taken a stricter program rather than the liberal, unstructured program which she decided on. She wonders if she should drop out of college and work for awhile; note too that she is not sleeping well, and so she gets a new, large prescription of sleeping medication.

The reader can see that Esther is burnt-out, adrift, and ripe for a major nervous breakdown. This girl is ill with indecision; she is swamped with ideas, but she cannot focus on a single idea. She cannot organize herself, or even organize a simple plan of action for her remaining summer weeks. She is drowning in her confusion, and there is no one there to lead her – not even a Fascist-type person like Marco. She has no disciplinarian, absolutely no one, and not a soul whom she feels understands her. She has returned Buddy's letter with only a catty scrawled note written in the margin. She is convinced that she has no friends – except her sleeping pills.

If a tissue of lies and disappointments surround Esther, then, the one defect in herself that she keeps focusing on is her unpreparedness for her future. She realizes that she doesn't know the poem *Beowulf* as well as most English majors do, and she wonders if her special scholastic privileges were what she really needed. Thus, it is not just indecision about what to do with her summer, or with her life, that is affecting Esther. She is starting to question every path and every experience of her life. She has skipped the regular scholastic requirements, and especially the courses in eighteenth-century literature, with "all those smug men writing tight little couplets and being so dead keen on reason." Now she wonders if she should have had the requirements, and the reader, at this point, surely wonders if Esther herself couldn't do with a bit of reason.

Esther saw a play in New York City, near the end of her stay, and its main character was a girl who was possessed by a dybbuk, or wandering soul. After Esther's date with Marco, we wonder what it is that "possesses" Esther – because Esther does not seem to use even the modicum of sense and wit that she had previously. As she tosses her fashionable wardrobe off the parapet, into the darkness of New York City, Esther also, besides freeing herself from "fashion," allows pieces of her sanity to fly away too. The darkness of the metropolis has her in its grip, and Esther has fallen into despair, from the arms of a brutal womanhater into the grayness of the night of indecision and non-direction.

Concerning the many problems that have led Esther to this state of confusion and indecision, note in particular the double standard that has been bothering her for a long time. The fact that the rules are different for men than for women does not seem fair to her. Even the execution of the Rosenbergs accents that sense of how America is prejudiced and how it lacks fair play. Esther feels victimized and helpless. She sees herself as a young, sensitive, creative woman headed in directions not prescribed by society, which only mouths ideas about freedom, opportunity, and equality.

Esther has seen the dark heart of America, and now she is lost in her own dark reactions. She can find no relief in her mother's suburban house, where she is constantly being condescended to and treated like an invalid – even before she is really sick. The nosy neighbor depresses Esther with her attempts to make everyone miserable while she herself conforms to "the system." And the other neighbor, lost in a fog of childbearing, does not give Esther relief from her dilemmas either. These extreme female roles, one mean and narrow, the other expansive and warm and mothering, are two opposite kinds of prisons that women are pushed into by a society that does not allow them any human roles – only roles fit for the "weaker" sex.

If these are the choices which are offered to Esther, it is no wonder that Esther cannot make a decision. Additionally, being rejected from the writing class makes her feel even worse; the one role in which she has sought and done well in is denied her, right now in her crisis. Esther's depression worsens, and her inability to sleep has aspects of manic behavior. Soon she can't even read. So it is recommended that Esther see a psychiatrist. Her dream of "a great summer" has hit bottom.

CHAPTERS 11-14

Struck with inertia, unable to choose anything constructive to do with her summer in the Boston suburbs, Esther is in limbo. Chapter 11 begins with a description of Dr. Gordon's waiting room, and Chapter 12 begins with a description of the waiting room of his private hospital. Esther is waiting, waiting for the verdict, the diagnosis of her life. But who will give the verdict, the diagnosis? Certainly not the suave, handsome doctor, nor can Esther's dutiful but befuddled mother.

"Suppose you try and tell me what you think is wrong," Dr. Gordon asks Esther. But Esther cannot even figure out the question, much less answer it. Esther is suffering from extreme depression and has symptoms of a variety of other mentally ill states. She is not sleeping. She has not washed her hair nor her clothes since returning from New York City, and she is still wearing Betsy's borrowed clothes. She wants Dr. Gordon to be fatherly and when he is not, she cannot relate to him. She writes to Doreen, then tears the letter into little pieces. Indecision. She goes out with a sailor but tells him that her name is "Elly" and says that she is an orphan from Chicago. Thus, she wants another identity. When a woman resembling Mrs. Willard walks by, she becomes anxious and paranoid.

On her second trip to Dr. Gordon, he suggests electro-shock treatments on an out-patient basis. He assures Mrs. Greenwood that she'll "have her daughter back" soon. Meanwhile, Esther is reading lurid scandal sheets and is intrigued by the story of a man who almost commits suicide by jumping from the seventh floor of a building; he is finally helped to safety by a policeman.

Esther analyzes in detail the matter of killing oneself by leaping. The seamy side of life and violence and death fascinate her, partly because all her family ever read was the *Christian Science Monitor*, a newspaper which Esther claims treated such things as "if they didn't happen." Even when Esther goes to Boston's Public Garden, she analyzes things in the most negative light. She decides that the Weeping Scholar Tree *must* have come from Japan, and then she goes into a long reverie on the merits of disembowelment. However, she concludes, she hates the sight of blood.

All of Esther's thoughts lead to suicide, it seems. And then, to make matters worse, Dodo Conway and Esther's mother drive her to Dr. Gordon's hospital in the Conways' hearse-like car. Gray images have now turned to black. Significantly, we only get the description of the Conway car after Esther has received her first shock treatment. We, as readers, almost wish that Esther had run away to Chicago, or that she had started hitchhiking somewhere. However, Esther always returns home – after her fantasies of escape – and thus she continues to be "a dutiful girl," following Dr. Gordon's plans, and doing as her mother and society think best.

One of the reasons why Esther always goes back home is that she feels she is "hopeless at stars" – and although she can find directions on a map, she can't understand them when she is lost. She also tends to lose track of time and frequently discovers that it is "too late." Her depression is now complicated by a definite sense of disorientation.

Dr. Gordon's private office is decorated in monochromatic beige, with green plants. The private hospital is also very chic and makes Esther think of a guesthouse in Maine. This sense of fashion is attractive to her. But both places have an air of unreality. The office is icily air-conditioned and windowless; the private hospital, in spite of its secluded drive, is white with quahog shells, and its light, summer resort appearance, is peopled with motionless human bodies, who have almost uniform-looking faces. Finally, Esther sees that some of the people in this institution are making "small, birdlike gestures," yet her final conclusion is that she is in a department store, surrounded by mannequins.

As Esther follows Dr. Gordon and prepares to undergo her first electro-shock treatment, she sees a shouting, struggling woman being dragged along the hall by an unsympathetic nurse with a medicinal smell. This wall-eyed nurse tells Esther that everyone is "scared to death" before their first shock treatment. When it is time for Esther's treatment, her temples are covered with grease, and Dr. Gordon fits two metal plates, one on each side of her head, with a strap. When Esther bites down on the wire which he gives her, she is shot through with "air crackling with blue light," and the jolts and flashes that split her body make her wonder "what terrible thing it was that I had done." Later, as Esther sits in a wicker chair holding a glass of tomato juice, after her "punishment," she remembers the time when she received a blue, flashing shock from a defective cord on a lamp beside her mother's bed. The scream that she emitted then was "like a violently disembodied spirit." Dr. Gordon asks her how she feels, and Esther lies and says, "all right." She can remember which college she goes to, and he is satisfied. Her disembodied spirit is not strong enough to rebel against him, to reject the institutions which ultimately seem to fail to protect and help her. On the way home in Dodo Conway's car, Esther experiences a feeling in which her mind seems to be sliding off into empty space, and after she is home she tells her mother that she is not going back to the hospital. Her mother, in classic denial fashion, smiles and says, "I knew my baby wasn't like that."

Back home, Esther becomes fixated on stories about a starlet who committed suicide, and her own demonic voices begin to chide her about her work and her neuroses. She is afraid that she'll never get anywhere. So she toys with her package of Gillette razor blades. She goes to the bathtub because a Roman philosopher had said it would almost be pleasant to open his veins in a warm bath. But Esther can't slit her own white, defenseless skin, so she packs up her blades and catches a bus to Boston.

Esther seeks directions to go to Deer Island. She weeps a few honest tears, and she finally gets the proper instructions. Before Esther's father died, the family lived on this island. It was an island then, but it is now connected to the mainland. Only a prison is out there now. Esther meets a guard, and ponders how her life would be if she'd married him and had a large family. As she sits by the sea, a small annoying boy comes up to talk to her. She is about to bribe him to go away when his mother calls. Esther is left to think about a cold sea death. But as the icy water reaches her ankles, she winces and picks up her things and leaves.

Chapter 13 begins with another beach scene. This time, Esther is lying on a brightly colored towel beside a boy named Cal. She thinks that her mother telephoned Jody and that's how this blind date was arranged. Cal is discussing what appears to be an Ibsen play; the chapter begins with Cal saying, "Of course his mother killed him."

Esther, however, is only interested in the play because there is a mad character in it, and she remarks, "Everything I had ever read about mad people stuck in my mind, while everything else flew out." Cal is intrigued with his "Yes" interpretation of the play while Esther wants only to know what the mother is going to use to kill the son. (She remembers, of course, but she wants Cal to *say* it—another case of Esther's intellectual dishonesty—"morphia powders.") Then Esther asks Cal how he would kill himself if he were going to do it. He says that he'd blow his brains out with a gun. This disappoints Esther because his answer is "just like a man," and she knows that she can't get a gun. She then reviews all the pro's and con's of using a gun and decides against that.

Jody and her boyfriend are happy together and that so unnerves Esther that she talks Cal into swimming with her. She wants to swim out to a rock, but Cal thinks that she is crazy and turns back. Esther keeps swimming, saying "I am I am I am." At this point, we learn that Esther tried to hang herself that morning and failed because ceiling beams and light fixtures in the house were unavailable. She returns again to thoughts of the past and to thoughts about her grandmother's house, where there were high ceilings. We also learn in this reverie of Esther's that she has been reading paperbacks about abnormal psychology and thinks that her case parallels the most hopeless cases. She worries about her family's lack of money and now, because she is a hopeless mental case, she fears that she'll end up in a terrible state hospital, hidden away. She tries to drown herself in the sea, but she keeps bobbing to the surface, as if the depths will not take her. She gives up and turns back to join her companions.

At this stage, Esther is unable to do anything right; she can't even kill herself with any of the traditional methods. When Esther's mother gets her a job as a volunteer in a hospital, Esther botches that too. She hopes that she will be assigned to work with some pathetic cases so that she can begin to feel that she herself *is* lucky — as her mother has moralized. However, Esther is, ironically, put in charge of handing out vases of flowers in the *maternity ward*. Here again, we see the theme of babies and children, a matter which depresses Esther very much. Esther tries harder at her job (but Esther has *always* tried harder and, for that reason, she is now mentally ill); and she rearranges the flowers, throwing out the dead ones and making all the vases look more attractive, and she practically starts a riot in the ward. She louses up one woman's yellow roses and throws out another's dead larkspurs. But instead of arguing her point with the women, Esther runs away and discards her green uniform as she goes.

The next scene shows Esther going to the graveyard where her father is buried, behind a Methodist church. She remembers that her mother had been a Catholic before his death, and Esther thinks that she wants to become a Catholic because the Catholic Church might have a way to persuade her not to commit suicide. Her mother, however, has laughed at Esther and said she would have to learn the Church's catechisms—one can't just suddenly "become a Catholic." Esther concludes that it's probably true; besides, priests are terrible gossips. Then she begins to remember a story about an insane nun. Her mind wanders back to her father and his neglected grave and all the things he would have taught her if he had lived. She can't find her father's grave and as she searches for it, she recounts her problem of trying to buy a waterproof raincoat that morning. She decided to buy a black one, but it is not waterproof and she is now damp and feels clammy. Finally, Esther finds her father's gravestone; there, she arranges a bouquet of azaleas that she picked near the entrance, and then she collapses in tears. She remembers that she has never cried for her father before. Her mother has not cried either; she has said that his death was all for the best because he would have rather been dead than a cripple. We see here how much Esther's mother has influenced her. Esther has not been able to mourn, and she has been pondering how she herself would be better off dead—than living in this less-than-perfect state. Perfection is all, it seems. "I laid my face to the smooth face of the marble and howled my loss into the cold salt rain."

However, Esther's tears come too late and perhaps are too few because in the next scene, she carries out a suicide attempt. She wants to join her father. And she actually goes through with this plan. She leaves a note stating, "I am going for a long walk," then she gets the key to unlock the strongbox where her sleeping pills are kept and seizes the new bottle (she'd plotted that it would take too long to save up enough, so this is the only way; Esther's mind is always cleverly plotting every detail), gets a glass of water, and goes down to the cellar, where she crawls under a breezeway addition to the house, and puts the logs back across the opening to lock herself in. She takes the pills, one by one, and finally she starts to see flashing red and blue lights. She sees the wreckage of her life in front of her, at the "rim of vision," then she is swept off, as if in a tide, to sleep.

Chapter 14 begins in darkness. Esther is in a cocoon-like silence; someone is moaning, and Esther feels cool winds and weights and then she feels a chisel on her eyes. Is she in an underground chamber? A voice cries, "Mother!" Then she feels warmth on her face. She opens her eyes but she can't see, and a cheery voice tells her that she'll marry a nice blind man someday. Later, when Esther tells the doctor that a nurse told her that she is blind, he says, "Nonsense," and tells her that she is lucky to be alive and will be fine. Esther's mother comes to see her because, she says, she had been told that Esther called out for her; then Esther's brother asks her how she is. Esther replies, "The same."

Esther's next visitor is the asylum's houseman, a fellow named George Bakewell, who was only slightly acquainted with Esther from her activities in church and at college. Esther becomes angry (at least, the reader thinks so), and she tells George to get out. But Esther is not angry; she has only turned her face to the wall because she thinks that George wants to see how a crazy girl looks. Esther then asks for a mirror, and against the nurse's wishes, she takes it and breaks it.

Esther is taken by ambulance to a state medical hospital where they have a "special ward" for her kind; it is implied that Esther is too violent to remain where she is. In this new institution, Esther encounters a Mrs. Tomolillo who has been hospitalized for sticking her tongue out continuously at her French-Canadian mother-in-law. When Mrs. Greenwood comes to visit Esther, this strange woman starts to mock Esther's mother, but Mrs. Greenwood doesn't notice. She is worried only about why Esther won't cooperate with the doctors—who are called Doctor Syphilis and Doctor Pancreas by Esther because she can't remember their real names. Esther tells her mother to get her out of this place, and her mother says that she'll try if Esther will promise to "be good." "I promise," Esther says in a loud, conspicuous voice.

The next two scenes give us a humorous but chilling view of a large state mental hospital. A Negro man is serving the patients some food out of tin tureens, and Esther perceptively sees that he has never encountered "crazy people" before. At the dinner table one day, Esther removes the lid from a container and takes some green beans; she passes it to the woman—Mrs. Mole—next to her, and then Mrs. Mole dumps the whole thing on her plate and then is led away by a nurse. The other foods they receive are baked beans and cold, sticky macaroni. When the Negro waiter and Esther exchange words, she kicks him in the leg.

In the next scene, Esther is in bed and doesn't want to get up. When a nurse sets a tray of thermometers on her bed, Esther (accidentally, on purpose) shoves them off so that they all break. This naughty scene takes place just after Esther has thought how she'd like to explain that she'd rather have something wrong with her *body* than something wrong with her mind. But it seems too tiring to try to explain, and the medical personnel are only custodians, anyway. After they lock the door, Esther scoops up some gray mercury to play with. These little separate pieces of mercury can, seemingly, be pushed into a whole again. Esther smiles at the silver ball and wonders what they have done with Mrs. Mole, the lady who dumped the green string beans. The point is clear: people's minds are not as easy to make whole again as droplets of gray mercury are.

Esther has gone from inertia and depression into attempting suicide, and in four chapters we see in graphic detail how her mind is working—especially on various ways to kill herself and the features of her environment and the people around her. But Dr. Gordon's original question of "what is wrong" has not even begun to be answered. We see that Esther's father's death has affected her very deeply, and that her mother's nurturing is, for the most part, only an exercise in duty. But why cannot Esther get herself beyond the details and find a reason for an existence? The mercury may be silver, but things are still dull and gray for Esther—in spite of her cleverness.

In these chapters following Esther's terrible depression, we see that Esther is able to rebel a little by breaking the thermometers. She takes satisfaction in being a little mean and somewhat clever, and we are reminded of the earlier scene in the novel when Buddy looks at Esther's broken leg with some sadistic satisfaction. We are also reminded of the time when Hilda was so cruelly satisfied about the Rosenbergs' executions. Esther hates that kind of cruelty, yet her own kindness is more often than not just passivity. And certainly her summer of sickness is an exercise in masochism.

Since Esther's friends are not people whom she can genuinely admire or feel close to, Esther is often in need of intimates—but she has none. After her self-destructive period, her notions of how to be well are laced with actions of clever deviation. In the scene where Esther tries to drown herself, but keeps bobbing back up, she says, "I knew when I was beaten." Here, the implication is that she is beaten by nature, which is forcing her back up to life. Yet it is *society*—not nature—that has beaten Esther; it has encouraged her cleverness, but cleverness is not genuine intelligence, and Esther has not realized that, as a woman, she does not *have* to be a passive creature. How, we wonder, can Esther be such a clever dummy?

When she is taken to Dr. Gordon's hospital for an electro-shock treatment, she notices that the people do not look real, that they appear to be mannequins. This is, of course, extremely upsetting. The hospital that is supposed to help people is turning them into zombies. This is darkly ironic because Esther's problems come from being too passive *already*. She should have just hitchhiked to Chicago—but, instead, she went home, as always, "like a good girl." The complexity of her situation is not understood by her doctors, who also do not understand her illness very well—in medical or in psychological terms, for just as Esther had waited, waited passively, in Dr. Gordon's office, now she is waiting for others to treat her, to cure her. When she wakes up, after her pill-taking suicide attempt, she thinks that she is blind. And in a way, Esther *is* blind because she doesn't know what to do, or which way to turn. Except for the pain of the electro-shock treatments, she could easily become a zombie also. She is at the mercy of her caretakers, who do *not* understand her.

When Esther first talked with Dr. Gordon, she felt that she was in "a black, airless sack with no way out," but she couldn't tell him about it. It is in this section of the novel that Plath first tells us what a bell jar is, and we note immediately that Dr. Gordon's office is windowless. Esther is in a windowless place, suffocating, and the doctor is *not* helpful. It must be noted here that Esther's serious suicide attempt takes place after she sees Dr. Gordon and after her first electro-shock treatment. Esther obviously does not feel that the doctor can help her, and she feels that she would rather die than be subjected to treatments that punish her body by making her feel that her bones are breaking and that her "sap" is flying out of her.

Again Esther is very worried about being hopelessly crazy and becoming institutionalized or being a "shop dummy" that will burden her family for life. Her thoughts of suicide go hand-in-hand with her reading yellow journalism articles on suicides and her conviction that she is a hopeless case. All of her attempts to feel better go awry. When she goes to the beach for freedom and solace, she discovers that she is on prison property. Windowless rooms, airless sacks, prison property, the bell jar. It is no wonder that Esther crawls into a hole and takes pills. Her life is a tomb anyway.

Ironically, one of the sickest people at the hospital that Esther is in, after her suicide attempt, is named Mrs. Mole, who turns the tureen of beans upside down on her plate and then is led away. Esther is left to wonder, "I couldn't imagine what they had done with Mrs. Mole." The real question, however, is: what will they do with *Esther*? Will her mother be able to help her? When will Esther take charge of her own life?

CHAPTERS 15-18

The next four chapters describe Esther's psychiatric treatment at a private hospital, arranged and paid for by Philomena Guinea. Chapter 15 begins with Esther riding on gray plush seats in Mrs. Guinea's black Cadillac. We learn that Mrs. Guinea herself was, at one time, in an asylum also, and that she has inquired to find out if Esther's case involves a boy. Mrs. Greenwood has told her "No," which is true, but as the four chapters evolve, we see that part of Esther's problem does involve conflicts about sex. Esther is very dependent on dates with men if she is to have a good self-image.

As they ride along in the luxurious car, Esther's mother sits on one side and Esther's brother sits on the other; thus, Esther is prevented from jumping out of the car. Esther sinks back into her feelings of nothingness and tells us about her 'bell jar,' where she is trapped. She believes that she'd be in her own sour air in this bell jar, even if she were in Bangkok. We learn that the private hospital where she is going is adjacent to the big state hospital. This is our first clue about her new treatment. And it is not long before we see that Esther is still plotting new ways to kill herself.

When we meet the director of the hospital, we realize that Esther is again to be subjected to an institution that will try to mold her and train her. Two chapters later, Esther tells us herself that at least she is comfortable here, implying that the new treatment is perhaps no more effective than at the state hospital. Here, the patients seem to have more golf and badminton, etc., and more attention is paid to fashion magazines. Is this, then, only a class difference? Dr. Nolan, Esther's new doctor, is a pleasant, understanding woman who assures Esther that her previous electro-shock therapy was not done properly. We discover that Esther is to be given insulin therapy, which will make her fat and, at some point, it is supposed to induce a reaction somewhat like electro-shock. Is this enlightened medical practice?

Esther has met two patients here. One is Miss Norris, who never speaks, and one is Valerie, who, we soon learn, has had a lobotomy.

It is clear that "all of the most sophisticated treatments" are used in this hospital. At the end of Chapter 15, we find Esther moving up to the front of the ward where there is more sunlight. Miss Norris is moving back to Wymark. She is not progressing. And progress is the key to comfortable quarters. Esther has kept Miss Norris company for many hours, and yet this lady has never said a word. Into all this gloom, a person from Esther's past recognizes Esther and calls out. It is Joan Gilling, who is also a patient at the hospital.

Chapter 16 gives us an account of Joan's illness, and we see that she has had many experiences like Esther's and also that many of their perceptions are similar. In addition, Joan has collected newspaper clippings that tell about Esther's disappearance and attempted suicide and rescue. They are like two little girls in a conspiracy with each other against a cruel and insensitive world. Joan has collected her clippings in much the same way that Esther collected yellow journalism articles.

Esther has her first insulin reaction, and Dr. Nolan tells her that she will not be plagued by any more visitors. Esther then tells us that on her birthday, Mrs. Greenwood brought her roses; she threw them out, then told Dr. Nolan that she hates her mother. Dr. Nolan replies, "I suppose you do."

Chapter 17 begins with Esther's being told how lucky she is. She is moving up to Belsize. Esther feels, however, that she is not ready for that. Belsize is a hospital where the patients dress fashionably, where they play bridge, but even if it is more comfortable, the competition is fierce. One of the patients is a Mrs. Savage, who has been to Vassar. Plath could not have told us much more about Belsize in many pages of description. "Savage from Vassar" is all we need to know.

It is at Belsize that Esther experiences her first treachery from the chic, cigarette-smoking Dr. Nolan. One day, Esther does not receive breakfast. She fears that this means that she is due for electro-shock treatment. But, she goes to the kitchen to protest the mistake and claim her meal. When it becomes clear that there *is* no mistake, she is furious because Dr. Nolan has promised to tell her and discuss the treatment with her. Dr. Nolan arrives, early, to take Esther up for the treatment. The trust between the two women is temporarily lost, however, because Dr. Nolan wanted Esther to sleep.

Esther now feels that she is in a white cocoon, unlike the dark one after her suicide, and the electro-shock treatment does not seem as painful and terrible as before. This time, Esther goes into a sleep, and she tells Dr. Nolan afterwards that the treatment was just like the doctor said it would be. Somehow, the reader is not so convinced of the humanity of these treatments.

The college dormitory atmosphere of Belsize shows us that Esther is still struggling with institutions, for when we see Esther coming out of her treatment with Dr. Nolan at her side, we remember Jay Cee and the *Ladies' Day* editorial offices. Esther has met these successful, helpful women before, but she has never been helped. Even Valerie, the girl scout-type with the lobotomy reminds us of girls from other phases of Esther's experience. Are each of these serial experiences, dealing with one kind of institution or another, rather like the one before? Are the new shock treatments just another program for Esther, not so different from the classes at college or the fashion workshops in New York? When will real learning or real change take place? Is Esther not only caught in the sour air of her own bell jar, but also in the sour air of failing institutions and failing cultural ideals that, somehow, cannot give her true sustenance, cannot give her any real support at this fragile time of her life?

At this point, Joan appears with a letter from Buddy Willard. But Esther has already received a letter too. Joan liked the Willards, but she stopped seeing Buddy's parents when Buddy started to date Esther. Esther thinks of telling Buddy that there is no one else – that he is simply the wrong one. We wonder if she has the strength to reject Buddy since having a boy friend is so important to her.

Esther recounts the morning scene when she accidentally walked in on Joan and DeeDee in a lesbian embrace. Here, we learn that Joan has been Esther's "secret sharer," but now Esther discusses with Dr. Nolan the fact that she can't understand homosexuality. She remembers a similar incident at college, and then she also recalls that when she told a female classical scholar that she might want to have children, this professor protested, "What about your career?"

Esther is clearly having many doubts and conflicts about her female role. But instead of thinking about that, she just goes and tells Joan that she doesn't like her and that Joan makes her sick. The resolution, for the time being, is a visit to a gynecologist in order to purchase a diaphram. Dr. Nolan has referred her to a doctor after a discussion with Esther about chastity, the subject of an article written by a woman lawyer. Dr. Nolan says that this is all propaganda, and she tries to help Esther to gain some sense of freedom. Esther thinks if she does not have the notion of a baby hanging over her head like the blade of a guillotine, she can be as sexually free as a man; she will finally be able to get well. So Esther gets her diaphram, and she thinks that all she has to do is find the right man to aid her in getting rid of her virginity, as if her illness were caused by that.

What we see again in these four chapters is that Esther's *symptoms* are being treated rather than her disease. Just as Esther's mother had urged her to go to school or do volunteer work or take up shorthand, and just as Jay Cee had urged her to do her editing tasks, and just as the old-style feminist professor had urged Esther to pursue a "career," now her liberated lady psychiatrist has given her "humane" shock treatments and the latest insulin treatments. And now she has sent Esther off for the best contraceptive available. All this may help Esther to live, on the surface, more comfortably, but Esther's real dilemmas and real troubles are never confronted.

The reader sees that there are only two short chapters left for Esther to find herself, for Esther to grow up, for Esther to begin to be well. Can she do it? Where are the resources to really aid her in this task of coming back from a deep underground cocoon to life?

In these four chapters, Esther's problems become more clearly defined, and we see the help that various people are trying to give her, however limited. Mrs. Guinea is paying for the best psychiatric care available, but is also complaining that it is not doing Esther enough good. It is to be wondered, here, if money and privilege are really that advantageous. Are these treatments helping Esther that much?

Esther was living in a fog, in her "bell jar," for some time before her suicide attempt, and we see that she had problems with disorientation. She was perceiving her existence in warped ways, and she was unable to function. But would she not have come out of this state as well by herself, as with the insulin and the electro-shock treatments? Did these treatments not prolong her dependence on institutions that did not understand her and increase her alienation? In any psychiatric situation, treatments which do not promote self-sufficiency are to be questioned. In addition, to believe that solutions to the problem are outside the individual rather than an internal process should also be suspect. Why was Esther not allowed to rest, just rest, after her suicide attempt?

We might say that these chapters show us not only Esther's problems, but also society's problems. There is a great deal of potential for good things to happen but because of a lack of common sense, because of the emphasis on quick achievement and competition, much is lost – including Joan's life, and we might add, eventually Plath's.

Perhaps the most important minor figure here is the one named Savage, from Vassar. The spectacle of the well-bred, well-dressed, bright young woman achieving everything and at an incredible pace is one of the most destructive parts of Esther's life. Nowhere in the novel does anyone suggest that Esther should be trained to slow down, to pace herself, to relax, to gently come to terms with herself – perhaps even over the years of a lifetime.

As helpful as some of the women characters try to be, their vision is not broad enough, nor does it encompass the best priorities. We never learn how, or why, Mrs. Guinea can cope with her life. She brings nothing to Esther except money; her "help" is negated by another message – namely, that success is the goal. But how? No one ever counsels Esther on how to survive. Jay Cee has advised concentration on work and studying more languages, and even though we might agree that work can be helpful to people, Esther seems overworked and over-wrought from it. Dr. Nolan helps Esther get contraceptive advice, suggesting that she thinks that sexual anxiety is at the root of Esther's problems. None of these solutions help the young Esther, however, and we might say that they actually encourage what is wrong with her – that is, compulsive ideas about success and sex.

When Dr. Nolan explains to Esther that women find tenderness in each other and that men do not give tenderness to women, we agree that that is a fairly valid observation, especially for the 1950s. But the women in this novel do not exhibit *enough* tenderness and understanding towards one another. They are only able to be partly supportive to Esther. And it is not because they lack the impulses for kindness. They lack wisdom and sense and true independence from society.

CHAPTERS 19 & 20

Joan declares that she's going to be a psychiatrist, as she and Esther sip apple cider. Their relationship is deteriorating, and Esther is envious because Joan is going to move into an apartment with Nurse

Kennedy in Cambridge. Esther is "staying on at the asylum," as Plath insists upon calling the mental institutions described in her book. Esther's doctors don't want her to live with her mother, and she has to wait for the winter term of her college to begin. During their conversation, Esther's mind drifts to her diaphram which lies in a bottom drawer of her dresser. When Joan asks Esther if she'll come and visit, Esther lies and says, "Of course."

Actually, Esther does go visit Joan, but the visit is not like either of them would have imagined. Esther has met a man named Irwin on the library steps and decides to go to bed with him. He is a professor of mathematics, and thus, Esther reasons, he is intelligent enough to be allowed to have sex with her. In addition, one of his "ladies," as he refers to them, appears on the doorstep while he is entertaining Esther, and she sees that this woman is a sensual Slavic type, so Esther feels that Irwin is sexually qualified for the job too.

Irwin takes Esther to a French restaurant, where she is greedy for butter and wine after the dull institution food that she's been eating. When Irwin seduces her, he is very surprised to discover that Esther is a virgin. The sexual act hurts Esther, but Irwin tells her, "Sometimes it hurts." After he finishes and goes to take a shower, Esther discovers that she is bleeding profusely. To try and stop the bleeding, she wraps towels between her legs and then has Irwin drive her to Joan's apartment.

After making several confused phone calls and not knowing exactly what to do, Joan takes Esther in a taxi to the emergency room of a hospital. There, a doctor declares Esther to be "one in a million," but he assures her that he can "fix" her.

Later, back at the asylum, Dr. Quinn, Joan's psychiatrist, comes to ask Esther if she knows where Joan might be. Esther thinks about how she wants to disassociate herself from Joan, just as she earlier wanted to disassociate herself from Doreen. Esther tells the doctor that Joan should be in her room at Belsize. As it turns out, Joan has hanged herself in the woods, near a frozen pond.

Chapter 20 begins with a description of the hospital and a description of Massachusetts, "sunk in a marble calm." There has been a fresh blanket of snow, and everything looks deceptively clean. In a week, if Esther passes her interview, she will be released from the hospital and will be transported to college in Mrs. Guinea's large black car. Dr. Nolan has tried to be realistic and warn Esther that people may treat her oddly. Mrs. Greenwood has characteristically brushed off the institutionalization as merely "a bad dream." Plath writes, "To the person in the bell jar, blank and stopped as a dead baby, the world itself is the bad dream." And in spite of all her treatments, Esther says that she remembers everything – cadavers, Doreen, the fig tree, Marco's diamond, the sailor, Doctor Gordon's wall-eyed nurse, the thermometers, "the Negro with his two kinds of beans," the extra pounds from insulin, and "the rock that bulged between sky and sea like a gray skull." Esther says that it's all part of her, part of her landscape.

When Buddy Willard comes to visit her, Esther has to shovel his car out of a snowdrift. The sun is starting to come out from behind gray clouds, and we think that Esther may actually be getting well. Buddy reveals his fears to us when he asks Esther if she thinks that *he* drives women crazy. Since he had also dated Joan, he is worried, but Esther assures him that he had nothing to do with Joan's suicide. He is relieved; he asks Esther with his characteristic insensitivity, who'll marry her now?

In the next scene, Esther calls Irwin to remind him of the emergency room bill that he neglected to pay. When he asks her when she'll see him again, she answers "Never" and hangs up. She says that his voice means nothing to her and now she feels "perfectly free."

We see Esther at Joan's funeral, wondering what she is burying. "I took a deep breath and listened to the old brag of my heart. I am, I am, I am."

In the last scene of the book, we see Esther leafing through an old *National Geographic* magazine, waiting for her interview. She is dressed correctly – in a red wool suit; her stocking seams are straight, but she has on her old, cracked patent leather shoes. She sees the silver-haired doctor who talked to her about pilgrims on her first day there, plus all the other faces, now without their masks. "The eyes and the faces all turned themselves toward me, and guiding myself by them, as by a magical thread, I stepped into the room."

So Esther leaves the mental institution, we assume, although we are never told that for certain. And certainly we never know if she was able to completely leave her bell jar. In fact, the room which she has just stepped into may be only another bell jar. The novel does not end with Esther's stepping into clear, clean air. Nor do we see her emerging with a new set of values for herself. Dr. Nolan has just guided her into another room.

When Esther steps into "the room" for her interview, hoping to be released from the mental hospital, the reader is reminded of Virginia Woolf's idea of "a room of one's own." It is odd that Esther has been studying James Joyce's works, but that Virginia Woolf's novels are never mentioned. Of all the women who might have helped Esther, Woolf is one whom we think of first. Woolf understood all that Esther is faced with, and she wrote brilliantly on so many aspects of being female, in modern society, as well as confronting madness.

But more than just a mentor, even the idea of "a room of her own" has not occurred to Esther Greenwood, and we wonder if, indeed, it occurred to Plath. Esther goes from room to room, rooms prepared for her by others, all geared to others' and the world's expectations. And all these places have been inadequate, and they have often been very cold. Esther's mother's house, Esther's father's academic life, her schools, New York City, and *Ladies' Day* magazine, and the hospitals – these have all been "rooms." Now, at the end of the novel, a board *room* will judge Esther's mental health.

Esther says that after hanging up on Irwin, she feels "perfectly free." But free of what? Her virginity? Men? Irwin? Her past? Remember that when her mother tells her, again denying any unplesantness in life, that they will put "all this" behind them, Esther knows that all these experiences are part of her, "part of [her] landscape," she calls it. Yet *where* is the landscape of escape? Where is solace?

Plath's husband, Ted Hughes, has said that the *Ariel* poems that Plath wrote during the last two years of her life have an authentic voice and reveal "a real self." We cannot doubt this. Even *The Bell Jar* proves this. But this real self, revealed in the novel as evidence of some very good writing, was written by a woman who never found a real life, who was never able to sustain herself in the real world.

Part of the answer to this tragedy lies in Esther's experiences and observations. She talks about Dr. Quinn, Joan's psychiatrist, as being too abstract. Yet Esther, in characteristic style, having the same defects as those whom she so bitterly criticizes, is certainly very abstract about the big event of her coming to womanhood – the loss of her virginity. She abstractly chooses the man who will go to bed with her – not for emotional reasons – but for made-up, clever, bright-girl reasons. And her desire to never see him again is quite abstract. Why? If Esther's mother wants to treat all experiences as though they were only "bad dreams," Esther also tries to brush aside that which was a mistake, that which she finds distasteful.

Clearly, Esther feels renewed at the end of the novel, for she wishes there were a ritual for being born twice. But she thinks of this in terms of marriage. She is not on new ground yet. Furthermore, in feeling so renewed, she seems to have accepted society's notion that she has been cured. Esther is still so young, so lacking in wisdom, so immersed in abstract ideas. She is still clever, still well-dressed, but not much more prepared for her future than she was at the beginning of the book.

CHARACTER ANALYSES

Buddy Willard

Buddy Willard is important to *The Bell Jar* because he is Esther's first real "boyfriend." He seems likeable, if a somewhat inept, young man who is working steadily toward his goal to become a doctor. His parents and Esther's parents have been friends and acquaintances, and it is clear that both sets of parents are in favor of this match. However, Buddy and Esther do not seem suited to each other, in spite of the fact that she has adored him from afar for some time, and Buddy, when he gets to know Esther, is enamored of her intelligence and her poetic sensibilities. Buddy has most of the attitudes of most of the males of his generation, including the notion that Esther will give up the idea of being a poet once she's had a baby. He introduces her to experiences at the medical laboratory and the hospital. He gets a poem published partly to show Esther that he is sensitive too. He does this after he has called a poem just "a piece of dust."

Esther is only truly happy with Buddy after she finds out that he is taking her to the Yale prom. That coup and her need for a boyfriend seem to be her major attractions to Buddy. Because of Esther's distaste for Buddy and because he comes to represent hypocrisy in men in general, and especially after he tells Esther of his summer affair with a waitress, his character is never developed fully. The reader sees him, for the most part, as a shallow, insensitive fellow, one who tries to initiate the innocent Esther into sex by suddenly undressing before her so that she can "see" a man. When he asks Esther if there is something wrong with him since both she and

Joan Gilling (one of Esther's girl friends) have attempted suicide, we see him again as an almost laughable figure.

Joan Gilling

Joan is from Esther's hometown, goes to the same church and is two years ahead of Esther in school. Joan is what Esther calls a "big wheel" – that is, she is president of her class, a physics major, and the college hockey champion. Joan is also a girl whom Buddy had dated before he takes Esther to the Yale prom. Buddy finds Joan to be a good sport, someone with whom he can do athletic things, and she doesn't have to be "pushed up hills."

As it turns out, Joan is very much the psychological double of Esther; they are both over-achievers; they are both unconventional young women. They both garner awards and succeed in their fields, and they both believe that they should try to become carbon copies of Mrs. Willard, the epitome of what a "successful wife" is in the 1950s. In addition, both girls attempt suicide, and both have woman doctors.

However, Joan is different from Esther. For one thing, she seems more impressionable and less critical of the influences around her. Joan loves Mrs. Willard, whereas Esther withholds her total admiration for anyone. Joan's field of study is physics, but after she has been in the psychiatric hospital, she wants to become a psychiatrist. She is in awe of Dr. Quinn, whom Esther describes as "a bright, shrewd, single lady," a person who gives Esther "the polar chills."

Joan is one of those athletic girls described in magazines of the 50s as being "horsey," and Esther is shocked to find her friend in a lesbian embrace with another girl in the hospital. Esther, herself, is tall and gangly, but she is not "horsey" and, certainly, she is not the typical feminine woman of the 50s.

Joan accompanies Esther to the hospital after Esther loses her virginity and can't stop the bleeding. After this experience, Joan returns to the mental hospital even though she had earlier been released; at that time, Esther was envious of Joan's "freedom" and of Joan's being "cured." Shortly after returning to the hospital, however, Joan leaves the grounds for the evening and never returns. She is found – hanging, in the woods. The reader never finds out what went wrong for Joan nor why she kills herself, whereas Esther, seemingly, recovers. Esther goes to Joan's funeral and repeats "I am, I am, I am." Significantly, Joan, Esther's peer and competitor, *is not*.

Mrs. Greenwood

Esther's mother is the most important figure in the novel after Buddy, the boyfriend, and Joan, the peer with a somewhat parallel fate. Mrs. Greenwood teaches shorthand, after Esther's father dies, in order to support the family. She stresses the need for having practical skills, and she tells Esther that even "the apostles were tentmakers." She is portrayed as having deep resentments toward her husband for not having provided properly for the family, as well as for dying early and leaving no insurance. Mrs. Greenwood is also pictured as a woman without much feeling. She works hard and expects her children to succeed, but there is not much display of warmth or emotion from her. Esther does not even remember her mother crying over Mr. Greenwood's death.

However, Mrs. Greenwood is a dutiful woman. When Esther comes home from New York City, Mrs. Greenwood sits with Esther in the evenings and tries to teach her shorthand; and after Esther's suicide attempt, she has Esther transferred out of the ugly state mental hospital by enlisting Mrs. Guinea's aid. Mrs. Greenwood wants to believe that her daughter "is not like those awful people," but, nevertheless, she tries to get Esther good medical care.

The relationship between Mrs. Greenwood and Esther never comes into great conflict, but it is never resolved either. The reader simply has images of Esther and her mother gliding from one place to another in gray or black vehicles, without leaving and without arriving.

The most significant matter that might be observed is that after Esther's first shock treatment, Mrs. Greenwood's knuckles are described as being "bone white, as if the skin had worn off them in the hour of waiting." Certainly, Esther's mother is a woman who has painfully, passively experienced the tragedies of her life without crying. By all social standards, she is a good woman, but Esther, it seems, wishes that – just once – Mrs. Greenwood would misbehave – or scream – or cry.

Doreen

One of the *Ladies' Day* girls, "Doreen came from a society girls' college down South and had bright white hair standing out in a cotton candy fluff round her head and blue eyes like transparent agate marbles, hard and polished and just about indestructible, and a mouth set in a sort of perpetual sneer." This Doreen, with her white hair and silky white items of apparel is another opposite of Esther. Her amused cynicism makes her quite indestructible – at least from Esther's point of view. Doreen does not take the magazine work seriously; she is in New York City to have *fun*. She takes Esther along on a date with Lenny, and she arranges the ill-fated date with the suave Marco, a date that has a devastating effect on Esther.

But Esther likes Doreen, even though she cannot be like her. What she likes most is the fact that Doreen is smart enough to see through the hypocrisies of society, and perhaps Esther is more than a little envious of Doreen's ability to make the best of a bad situation.

When Doreen gets drunk and vomits outside Esther's door, Esther just leaves her there on the rug and shuts the door. Esther is not able to take this double life of the white Southern belle. Yet when Esther leaves New York City, Doreen gives her a half suitcase of avocados to take home. We never hear of Doreen again. We do not know if wearing white and having fun worked better for her than Esther's wearing black and trying to be successful.

Betsy

Betsy is the *Ladies' Day* girl from the Midwest. She is truly innocent and sweet and has none of the cynicism of the southern Doreen or the New Englander Esther. She becomes a photographic model for the magazine and is portrayed as being healthy and cheerful. Doreen calls Betsy "Pollyanna Cowgirl." As a character, Betsy seems well brought-up, bright, and someone who will work hard enough to succeed and get what she wants. But Betsy is protected from seeing society and the world for what they are. Either she is not as smart as Esther, or she has psychological blindfolds on, or her cultural background prevents her from being critical. We do not know what happens to Betsy either, but she seems headed for the Miss America contest and a life of selling wholesome American products.

Jay Cee

Jay Cee is the editor of *Ladies' Day* magazine. She skillfully manages all the difficult people whom she has to deal with, and she does it diplomatically; she is a good manager and organizer. She wears suits, hats, and thick eyeglasses but tries to make herself more feminine with pastel-colored blouses and flowers (artificial) pinned to her hats. In general, she could be described as having bad taste. She sends telegrams to the girls after they become sick because of the tainted crabmeat at the magazine luncheon. When Esther falls behind in her work at the office, Jay Cee calls her in and gives her some advice. She suggests that Esther study languages as a key to becoming successful in the business of editing magazines or any other work in publishing. When the girls are being photographed, toward the end of their stay, Jay Cee wittily tells the photographer that Esther "wants to be everything."

Jay Cee's major function in the novel is that of a successful career woman, a woman, however, that Esther is not particularly interested in emulating – even if she is married.

Philomena Guinea

Mrs. Guinea is another adult model for Esther. She is not only a successful writer, but she is wealthy as well. She lives in a large mansion and lives well. At lunch, fingerbowls with little cherry blossoms are served, and Esther, thinking that she has been served "some clear sort of Japanese after-dinner soup," drinks it.

Mrs. Guinea, well-bred as she is, never really says anything to Esther. Mrs. Guinea's first novel was made into a movie with Bette Davis, and a long-running radio serial, based on the novel, is still running. Mrs. Guinea flies back from the Bahamas to help Esther be admitted into a good private hospital after her suicide attempt. Apparently, Mrs. Guinea is willing to pay for Esther's care since Mrs. Greenwood has told her that it is Esther's writing problems that have made her ill. For some reason, never explained, Mrs. Guinea would not have anything to do with Esther's case if it involved a boy. Mrs. Guinea keeps telling the doctors that she is not satisfied with their treatment of Esther.

Doctor Nolan

She is the third successful woman figure in the novel who tries to help Esther. She is a slim, young psychiatrist and works at the private hospital where Esther is given insulin and electro-shock treatments after she is transferred from the state hospital. Dr. Nolan is a kind, helpful therapist, but she is wrong not to consult Esther before her first shock treatment as she promised. Even though Dr. Nolan arrives early at the hospital, Esther already knows that she is due for shock treatment because she did not receive any breakfast.

Dr. Nolan tries to be warm and supportive, but she is not an intellectual equal of Esther, and Esther does not totally trust her. Dr. Nolan helps Esther by advising her about getting a diaphram, and, thus, in a practical way, she helps Esther with her fears about sex and getting pregnant. We suspect that Dr. Nolan encourages Esther to leave the hospital before Esther is ready to be self-sufficient, but otherwise one cannot fault this woman for trying to do her best, with the limited techniques and ideas available to her.

CRITICAL ESSAYS

Plath, the Individual, versus Society

It is obvious from her poetry, from *The Bell Jar*, and from her other writings that Sylvia Plath was an exceptionally intelligent and sensitive girl and woman. How was it, then, that as an individual she never found a comfortable, comforting, and nurturing place for herself in the world?

When we look at her childhood, we see that Plath's father encouraged her precociousness and that Plath's mother made great efforts to see that her daughter would be successful in society. She certainly came from a family that encouraged and rewarded her achievements and made it clear that discipline was one of the keys to success.

Was the ill-fated, short life of Plath really grounded in her father's untimely death when she was barely eight years old? She writes of this loss again and again, but never does she seem to be able to give up grief, or perhaps give into grief so that she can go on. Her grandfather, a seemingly kind person who gave her attention and companionship, never was able to fill the void left by her father. Yet Plath's father does not seem to have been so exceptional, especially as a father. At first, he was even disappointed that Sylvia was a girl, and he was not, initially, even interested very much in fatherhood. But Plath apparently made herself so charming that he was won over.

Much of the superficial character of Plath seems based, especially from a reading of *The Bell Jar*, on appearing intelligent, being witty and "with-it." Esther, and also Plath herself, it seems, wanted to be the bright girl whose accomplishments would be the envy of everyone. What this led Plath to was a certain kind of youthful narcissism that we find ultimately distasteful, a narcissism that probably did not help the poet Sylvia in her attempts to mature. For example, in 1958 Plath wrote a poem called "I Want, I Want," and we are struck with the idea that Plath wanted much from life and that she wanted it quickly.

If she never gave herself to mourning, as her mother never did (according to Plath's accounts of the tearless funeral), Plath, like a narcissistic person, never even gave herself wholly to her youthful desires. Thus, there is a thinness to even her own preoccupation with herself. We never find out just exactly what Esther can't stand about Buddy Willard, except that he is a hypocrite – by her terms.

Perhaps it is this immaturity which causes the youthful Plath to leap into the various stages of her life before coming to terms with the previous ones. Note that she throws herself into her academic work, but does not give up her childhood feelings. Then she takes off for New York City before she has been able to absorb her college experiences. After her breakdown, she finishes college and is off to England. Before we know it, she is married and working on her writing and her career. Then quickly she has two children, and then she is separated from her husband. And we learn that while she was in the United States in 1958 that she was seeing her psychiatrist again. All this is done very much like a child skipping from one rock to the next, never stopping for long. It is no wonder, therefore, that Esther was never able to make up her mind about which 'fig' to choose. Plath, in a similar way, was always too busy taking bites out of each fig to settle on one particular fig.

A work which gives us keen insight into the competitive nature of the women of Plath's place and time is Jane Davison's *The Fall of the Doll's House.* Davison's work is a social history of women in relation to their homes, their domiciles. What we learn from her about Plath is instructive, and, important to her study, Davison was a peer of Plath since they shared a dorm at Smith. Davison, in telling us about the women of the 50s – the ambitious, privileged ones who went to the "seven sister colleges" – paints a picture of young girls who wanted to be "tops" in everything. They wanted success in their careers, homes, and for themselves personally. They wanted to be bright and beautiful and rich. Davison tells us how Plath pored over women's magazines in an effort to write pieces that would sell. She quotes a letter in which Sylvia is writing home from England to her mother and begging for old copies of *Ladies' Home Journal* because she misses them so in London. Thus, we see that Plath didn't want to be just a good writer; she wanted to be a kind of perfect female who could decorate a house stunningly. And of course, she could not fill all those roles. No wonder she became bitter at times. If society was lacking, so was Plath's idea of her place in it. How exhausting.

This scattering of forces was based, perhaps foremost, in Plath's insecurity and also perhaps in a certain kind of romantic egotism. Sylvia could do anything, yet she never felt worthy of one, single, solid position in life.

This inability to be really connected to outside roles, or groups, is clearly seen in her relationship with her family and friends, and also in the scenes set in the mental institution in *The Bell Jar*. We wonder how Plath really did deal with her marriage to Ted Hughes, despite all the letters to her mother describing how well things were going; for many years, clearly Plath did not accept her life whole-heartedly, nor did she thoroughly reject it either. When Esther is to have her picture taken for the *Ladies' Day* "summer splash," Esther hides in the bathroom because she feels like crying. She finds her modeling role distasteful, but she doesn't say "no" either.

This kind of neurosis that afflicts especially the young (male and female) has been described by many writers. Some authors view it as immaturity and allow their characters to at last grow up; some see it as budding rebellion against an unjust society, but even then the characters must eventually take the world into account. Some see it as "the sickness of youth," and the outcome of the individual's life depends on the individual's character (plus fate and/or history). In *The Bell Jar*, we never see Esther getting beyond this intense preoccupation with herself.

Sometimes we wonder if this narcissism might be due to the fact that Plath's neurosis was simply the style then, a style that we also see in *Catcher in the Rye*, a novel of the same era. This inability to make choices, to decide on responsibilities, plus the scattering tendencies, the fragmentation – all these were responses to the overly rigid, conservative times of the 50s. Susan Sontag, in her book *Illness as Metaphor*, talks about cancer, but she makes the point that *society* decides the style of what consists of "tragic illness" and how its members will deal with the illness. Plath, in *The Bell Jar*, tells us much about the "style" of the time, and we realize that it is Esther's stint on the fashion magazines which, Plath seems to be saying, is responsible for Esther's breakdown.

We begin to wonder if Esther takes up mental illness partly because it is available to her and trendy. Then she gets caught in her game and becomes suicidal because she can't find a place for herself. Her narcissism has trapped her. She has pursued success and "happiness" to a dead end. She can't examine the past honestly, and she has no interest in the future. She can't internalize happy associations. She is an individual who is lost, adrift. Every idea for her future, in terms of jobs or roles, seems to be either distasteful to her or impossible to achieve. With that state of mind, expectations have not only diminished, but disappeared. Death, then, seems the only path, suicide the only role.

And even though Esther survives, as did Plath in her first suicide attempt, Esther is still lost and indecisive at the end of the novel. We can see from such poems as "Lesbos" and "Daddy" that Plath did *not* find motherhood and marriage to be roles that particularly suited and fulfilled her; in fact, her anger was quite intense because of these roles. These roles were like "institutions"–that is, they restricted and tormented her, just as school, the magazine, and the mental hospital did.

Plath should have made her peace with the institutions of society, or else developed ways to avoid them. Unfortunately, she got tangled up in her own narcissism and even though that may have sparked superlative poetry from her, in the end it was not self-protective. It was ultimately only self-absorbing and self-destructive. Clearly, it was only in poetry and in her own self-tortured darkness that Plath found a place for herself. And that place was not safe–or healthy. In her other social roles, Plath never found real absorption or completion. Initially, she may have felt fulfilled to have her two babies, one a girl and one a boy, but her poetry and *The Bell Jar* gives us too many negative images of the burdens of cleaning up after puking infants to make us believe that this could ever have been an accepted, part-of-motherhood job for Plath.

Plath was alienated. The institutions that she describes in *The Bell Jar* leave Esther alienated. Plath's father and his academic career gave her the idea that her relationship to society was to be determined by her success in school. And Plath did that – she was academically successful – but it did not make her happy; eventually she abandoned her academic teaching career at Smith. Then there is the portrait of the parents' marriage and the kind of household that her mother was in charge of after the father's death. As a parallel, Esther cannot embrace this role for herself, as she so clearly points out when she is talking about Mrs. Willard. Consider also the emptiness of the Boston suburb; this is what depresses Esther so much before her first suicide attempt. In *The Bell Jar*, Plath paints a very bitter portrait of her schools – at least the negative side that made her feel out of place.

Later, we encounter Plath's conflicts with institutions – that is, Esther's conflicts with the mental hospitals. Plath did not find a role – not even here. Unlike Joan, Plath did *not* want to become a female psychiatrist. Perhaps she was happier in England, at Cambridge, and after she married Ted Hughes, but her poem "Daddy" makes us question how right marriage was for Plath.

We see, through her portrayal of Esther, and from accounts of Plath's life, that she had a very difficult time finding comfort in traditional social roles, especially roles associated with traditional institutions. Supposedly, according to Plath's mother, there was to be a second novel which would tell the happy side of the same events of *The Bell Jar*. That novel, of course, was never written, and one reason why it was not written may have been because Plath was too alone in a world where only her poetry gave her relief.

We see Esther at the end of the novel going into the board meeting at the mental hospital. She is scared, and she feels unsure of herself. This is not the right place for her to be. "I stepped into the room," she says. The point is this: it is "*the* room." Plath never found *her* room, as in the phrase "a room of one's own" (from Virginia Woolf's long essay). Esther has progressed from her own bell jar to the board room, but it is "a place," a room, in an institution that is too insensitive, too unimaginative, too rule-bound, and too traditional for Esther to feel relaxed. We know now why she retreated to the bell jar. There, she was herself at least. There, she had authenticity. And there, she found a kind of comfort which the world's rooms never gave her.

In conclusion, Plath's narcissism was two-edged. She created and enjoyed it, but she never found a workroom that she was comfortable in, and enjoyed, and the world never showed her a better place to be. Plath herself, it should be noted, never pressured the world's institutions to serve her and to help *her*. We regret that that never happened and that Sylvia Plath didn't find a 'room' for herself where she could breathe freely and feel that Yes, *this* was her place, her role, her room.

What Went Wrong for Sylvia Plath?

This may be an impertinent question. There is the equally valid litany of "what went right?" because Plath left behind a collection of impressive poetry, a novel, a distinguished academic career, a marriage to an important British poet, and two children. She was not a stereotypically brilliant but eccentric "loner." Yet the shortness of Plath's life, plus her suicide, leads most of us to wonder about her tragic death.

Perhaps Plath was one of the first of the post-World War II, post-50s era women who lived lives of intensity, creativity, and success, and died early of some kind of self-abuse. Sensitive artists, frustrated by a world which they found cruel, demanding, seductive and bewildering – these poets, musicians, and artists of varying kinds, took excesses of different kinds of drugs. We witnessed the drug-related deaths of Jimi Hendrix and Janis Joplin, the suicides of Marilyn Monroe and the poet John Berryman, the alcoholism of many creative men and women, and in 1983 Karen Carpenter died of anorexia, refusing to eat, starving oneself.

We look to modern society for the sociological causes for these self-destructive phenomena, to the human mind for the psychological causes, and to the individual characters of the personalities involved for the specific reasons for the *early loss* of our creative spirits. In Sylvia Plath all these causes can be duly noted. But still we wonder: why? Is it not possible to have more specific answers, more scientific approaches?

One of the latest approaches to mental illness is physiological. It is now believed by a growing segment of the medical profession that serious psychotic disturbances, whether chronic or periodic in their manifestations, are caused by chemical imbalances in the brain and/or neurological systems. These various syndromes may be genetically, or chromosomally, transmitted. Manic-depression and schizophrenia are now suspected to run in certain families and are being treated with chemicals such as lithium with some degree of success.

The idea that any mental disorder is physically inherited is disturbing and frightening to many Americans, especially since our country has emphasized the psychoanalytical approach to curing emotional problems. One remembers Ingmar Bergman's classic film *Through a Glass Darkly*; there, a young woman is going mad, again, and we learn that her mother died in an institution for the insane. Scandanavia has long realized and accepted the notion that perhaps madness can be inherited. America is only now considering the theory, guardedly.

In the controversy over *cause*, however, we should not lose sight of remedies that alleviate or help control the condition. It is clear that psychoanalysis and psychiatric therapy have helped many people. Others claim relief from drugs and even electro-shock therapy. Soon we may have tests, taken from body samples, that will pinpoint specific deficiencies in the body that, when corrected, will lead the patient to renewed mental vigor. Currently some doctors do hair analyses to see if certain nutrients are lacking in a person's body. This and other methods, especially those related to the health food movement, are frowned on by the traditional medical profession. Yet the need for extra vitamin C and its usefulness in preventing colds, or even cancer, is a controversy that continues. Obviously, more scientific data is needed. Until then, sensitive persons can look only to themselves and follow paths of moderation and try to keep their own bodies and minds in balance by whatever means seem appropriate and useful to them.

Then there is the last period of Plath's life – when she had been seriously ill with flu for some time, and she was using drugs to get herself up and down for work and sleep. Certainly her body was not in any balanced, healthy condition at the time of her death. Did she ever eat or exercise properly? We have no real evidence that she did.

As I wrote these Notes, I consulted a Chicago psychologist – partly because I wondered if Plath might be a manic-depressive, depressed at certain periods and manic in her creative periods. His analysis was that the girl in *The Bell Jar* (and thus perhaps Plath herself) had endogenous depression, a condition thought to be congenital, or something one is born with. He pointed out that none of the events of Esther's life prior to the overdose of pills were traumatic enough to warrant her reactions and that the descriptions in the book outline a character who has been depressed for a very long time. Many readers of the book itself are struck by how depressing the story is. One student recently observed that not only is the girl in *The Bell Jar* depressed, but that the woman who wrote it was probably depressed.

An interesting aspect of Esther/Sylvia's mental problems as a young girl is that her behavior took the form of withdrawal and then depressive suicide. When one compares this to other examples of intelligent youths who are disturbed, one observes that often young males act out their problems aggressively in society, sometimes appearing criminally destructive, while Plath's female characters, Esther and Joan, hide in lonely self-destruction. A contrasting example is Alex, from a 1978 Norwegian film *Says Who?*. In this protest film, written, directed by, and starring Petter Vennerød, the young poet is angry at society's injustices and his own inability to find a good place in the world. Like Esther, Alex is very bright and sensitive, but he starts fights and is dragged off to mental hospitals while Esther just locks herself in her bell jars.

On the other hand, a 1983 Swedish film *Mama: Our Life Is Now*, by Suzanne Osten, uses the diary of Ms. Osten's mother, written from 1939-44, to give us a portrait of a young female film director. The artistic and egocentric Gerd, "Mama," wrote about a bell jar which she felt surrounded her. When Osten was asked about her mother's use of that image in an obscure diary that Plath could never have read, her response was, "This must be some common experience that women have." Whatever the causes of this bell jar depression and whether or not women experience it differently than men can, of course, never be determined absolutely, but certainly these two women have given us memorable accounts of what it feels like to be encased within a bell jar.

The difficulty of concluding what was wrong with Sylvia Plath resides, of course, in the complexity of Plath, as well as her situation, especially her situation as a woman, and the difficulty in any case of mental ill-health in determining the cause, much less the cure. Some day, there may be tests to determine chemical imbalances of the nervous system and specific remedies to right the body and mind. Until then, we must look at Plath's life as we would view any sad story and say that it was plagued by problems and some bad luck. For if she had had a different mother, or if her father had not died when she was young, if she had had more supportive female friends, if she had had different medical or psychiatric treatment, or different nutrition, would she be alive today? That is what tragedy is – the accumulation of many factors and causes which add up to a conclusion of futility. If we alter any one of them, the tragedy might not have occurred. The interesting question, then, is: *if* and *when* a cure has been found for various forms of depression, will that eliminate the tragedy of suicide? Probably not. But it might alter and prolong the emotional states and lives of certain sensitive people. For the present, unfortunately, we cannot discover what went wrong for Plath; we also cannot discover exactly what caused her creative output. We are left only with the portrait, the sometimes sketchy picture, of her life, with its early end. And, of course, we are left with its poetry, its art.

Anxiety About Death in *The Bell Jar*

One of the first observations one might make about *The Bell Jar* is that it is a book filled with fears about death. Even the bell jar itself is a suffocating tomb, an airless place where the soul dies, if not the body. Consider the first page of the book with its reference to the execution of the Rosenbergs and the speaker's inability to get a cadaver's head out of her mind—all these images and ideas point to what is perhaps the main preoccupation in the book: death.

When Esther wants Buddy Willard to show her "some really interesting hospital sights," this excursion includes a look at four cadavers and a number of glass bottles filled with dead babies. Esther is proud of how calm she is when observing these "gruesome things." She even nonchalantly leans her elbow on Buddy's cadaver while he dissects it. Later, watching a baby being born does not give Esther any sense of birth and life. She describes the baby as looking like a blue plum and is bothered by the fact that the mother is drugged into some, supposedly, painless state of oblivion.

Thus it is not really strange, thematically, that Plath's book soon starts to center on Esther's thoughts of suicide, on thoughts of death, for death-like images take precedence early in the book's plot, and they have been foremost in Esther's mind all along. Even when Buddy undresses before Esther, she tells him that she's only seen nude men as statues in museums, and her reaction to Buddy's genitals is that they look like "turkey necks and turkey gizzards"; this is humorous, but it reminds us that Plath has picked a death metaphor again for she sees Buddy's life-giving genitals as being similar to pieces of dead, gutted birds.

Plath's immersion in thoughts of death pervades the book and, indeed, there is a great deal of death in all of Plath's work. Likewise, Esther's anxiety about death takes precedence over all other of her anxieties about life. Esther, in fact, is so stricken with fear that she often can have no reaction at all to things that happen – except to lie. For example, when Buddy asks her how she liked watching the birth of the baby, she hedges, "Wonderful, I could see something like that every day." Yet she is, in reality, quite overcome by the "awful ordeal" that the woman must go through. And she is angered by the attitudes of the male doctors. Yet she expresses none of this, even to Buddy. Her fears and anxieties keep her from even expressing her own honest emotions. She buries those too, and thus with her lack of courage, she leads herself straight to depression.

The fear of death is the backside of the fear of life. And Esther, like a child, is fearful of life. By not expressing this and giving vent to her feelings, in some attempt to declare the validity of her reality, her life, she is thrust back to her fears and then to the ultimate fear: fear of dying.

This is more than merely a fear of death, or a fear of life. This is more than anxiety or depression. This is some kind of love for, or addiction for, one's own end. Perhaps this is truly the death instinct. And even though we might say that everyone has this and that anyone might succumb to it, given the right set of circumstances, some people – for example, Plath had this instinct pervasively and con- tinuously, and rarely does the life instinct overpower it.

In Ernest Becker's *The Denial of Death*, the author talks about transference and how people need this in order to attempt to make themselves whole from their fears and anxieties. However, transfer- ence is a distortion of reality. "But now we see that this distortion has two dimensions: distortion due to the fear of life and death and distortion due to the heroic attempt to assure self-expansion and the intimate connection of one's inner self to surrounding nature."

I conclude that Plath, in an attempt to deal with the great pain and anxiety of her life, focused her fears on the fear of death. This eventually became an obsession with her, and thus led to the suicide attempts. She did "attempt to assure self-expansion" by writing about her inner experiences. This is the heroic part of her life – the fact that she did produce good poetry, as well as the fact that she did struggle in an attempt to insure some kind of immortality. But she could not get past the death theme and on to her life impulses – at least Plath's writing does not show us that she could do that. A poem that she wrote in the month of her death shows Plath returning to "that cadaver's head . . . like some black, noseless balloon stinking of vinegar," an image which she mentions on the first page of *The Bell Jar*.

In her poem "Balloon," Plath tries to write about life, focusing on the Christmas holiday they have just celebrated and on the baby boy squeaking a balloon. Yet, in the end, the balloon is burst, leaving only a shred of red in the baby's fist. The poem's early images are disembodied, and then the end comes, with nothing. We recall the first lines of Plath's last poem, "Edge": "The woman is perfected./ Her dead/ Body . . . ."

Dr. Johnson, an English essayist of the eighteenth century, said that the prospect of death concentrates the mind. We see that principle operating in Plath in a perverse way. Her death thoughts, however, led to excellent poetry. But her poetry never became a path to freedom from those thoughts. We see that *The Bell Jar* was an attempt at self-analysis, perhaps an attempt for Plath to cure herself. Yet it did not work. She was able to transform her fears and phobias and obsessions into literature, yet the literature did not become a way for her to save herself. Was it just that the poetic gaze into the abyss was too much for Plath? Did she become too enamored with the abyss? Did the high of creativity, the drug of writing poetry make Plath think that she could escape the pain of life somehow, and when she couldn't, she turned that anger on herself? For some reason, Plath was never able to get beyond or above, or over, her childish fears of life and death, and maybe even her fear of sex. She was not able to get to that point where the adult knows that life is to be lived and lived as an act of faith, as an act of courage. One must at some point, eventually, decide to choose life, not death. At this point, death becomes an adversary. Death is *not* the "sweet drug," not a friend.

We sympathize with Plath, however, who became tired of her struggle. We remember how the death of her father, when she was eight, affected the rest of her life, and of how, when she was eighteen and troubled after her summer in New York City, she wanted only to join him in his grave. Clearly, Plath desired – sometimes more than death – a superior power, or force, to give form and authority and form, and thus a sense of happiness, to her early life. Then he was gone, and she tried to replace him, as she so bitterly tells us, in "Daddy": "I made a model of you,/ A man in black with a Meinkampf look." Her art was an attempt to give herself to something with a life force and a possibility for immortality. Yet, in the end, her death force won, and her anger that she expresses in the line "Daddy, daddy, you bastard, I'm through" is turned back on herself. Only death, ultimately, will not disappoint Plath.

Suicide – A Conclusion

Camus tells us, in *The Myth of Sisyphus*, that the single most important philosophical dilemma that human beings must face is the issue of whether to choose to end it all. Shakespeare, too, had posed the question in Hamlet's "To be, or not to be" soliloquy. Plath, perhaps the product of an era more inclined toward the "not," died by her own act.

In some ways, we, the readers, are left to judge not only Plath's action, but to evaluate the whole literary and cultural tradition that spawned her. First, there was Eliot's *The Waste Land*, and then there were several decades during which the best and brightest had only the most depressing things to say about life and the human condition. We were led from Prufrock to Norman Mailer's main character in *An American Dream*, a novel in which a man stabs his wife. Indeed, students of modern American literature often ask, "When can we read something more cheerful?" Coupled with this philosophical point-of-view was the phenomenon of the stream-of-consciousness narrative, a technique created by James Joyce and Virginia Woolf and used extensively by William Faulkner, three of the great writers of this era. It is no small accident that Plath was studying "the double" in Joyce's work as part of her honors program at Smith, for she mentions Joyce often in her journals and in her work.

What is important, for evaluating this whole literary tradition – from Eliot on – and important to a serious discussion of the problem of suicide, is why so many of the bright, young, classical school-of-thought students were more interested in Joyce and Eliot than they were in Woolf and Faulkner. And this is where we must place Plath, for certainly, even if she does not mention Eliot at length, her bell jar image is the direct descendant of his waste land; in relation to our contemporary polluted world, we now get clear air only within a bell dome.

In Woolf and Faulkner, the sensitive reader can find reasons to live as well as reasons to die. There is Septimus Smith (a suicide) in *Mrs. Dalloway* and Quentin Compson (a suicide) in *The Sound and the Fury*, but there is also Sally Seton and Mrs. Ramsey (lovers of life) in Woolf, and there is Dilsey and Dewey Dell, Addie Bundren, and Lena Grove and Isaac (all lovers of life) in Faulkner. We might conclude, therefore, that Plath either did not wish to hear, or did not hear, for some reason, the voices that said, "Live, live!"

There exists a sad quote from Plath's journals of the Boston period, 1958-59: "Take a lesson from Ted. He works and works. Rewrites, struggles, loses himself. I must work for independence. Make him proud. Keep my sorrows and despairs to myself. Work and work for self-respect. Study language, read avidly. Work. . . ." She wishes to take a lesson from another writer, and her desire to find a good role model is hampered by the complexity of the fact that she is married to Ted Hughes, another poet. She desires independence and self-respect, which she deserved, but side by side with that wish is a greater desire to make her husband proud. Thus, her compulsion is to work, work—for *someone else's* approval. In this single quotation, we can see a driven, lost human being in conflict. Plath searches for order only in books and work. Did she ever think that she might try to live, to exist, to wander down the road of life like Lena Grove in Faulkner's *Light in August*?

No wonder the paths of so many gifted writers of this period led to the mental hospital. And it should be noted here that both Kesey's *One Flew over the Cuckoo's Nest* and Hannah Green's (also a pseudonym for Joanne Greenberg) *I Never Promised You a Rose Garden* were published in 1963, the year in which *The Bell Jar* was published—and yet, of the three writers, only Plath committed suicide. It was due—at least in part—to Plath's work and her dramatic end that the early women's liberation movements in the United States were spawned. This led to a great surge of literary writing by women, a fact that should lead us to a serious contemplation of the major ideas of the era that preceded the new "freedoms" for women because only in a clearer understanding of that recent history will we avoid another time of tragedies for the Sylvia Plaths of the future.

In regard to this last issue, it is appropriate to look at the ethics of suicide. Perhaps it is even a time to re-read Aquinas on "The Sin of Suicide" because we should consider whether or not it was "wrong" of Plath to take her own life and leave two very young children in the world without a mother. Is it not ironic that Plath did to her own children what she was so damaged by in her own life – the loss of a parent at a tender age? And last, how are we to judge a woman who bitterly criticized her mother and idolized her father, yet she chose the self-destructive path of the father (and Otto Plath, although not a suicide, certainly contributed to his early death, as is clear from all accounts, because he refused to seek early medical treatment for diabetes) and then, in the end, did to her husband just precisely what her father had done to her mother? Indeed, it is ironic that in Plath's poem "Daddy," she foreshadowed how she herself would end her life. In this poem, she identifies her father as a Nazi figure and herself as a Jew. "I thought every German was you," she says, referring to her father. She then goes on to describe an engine "chuffing" her "like a Jew" off to Dachau, Auschwitz, and Belsen. Sharply foreboding in the next sentence, she writes, "I may be a bit of a Jew." Here, it is time for us to recall how Plath died: she gassed herself. It is as if she could not escape some almost foreordained doom for herself. This is indeed some kind of reverse, perverse, and hostile "poetic" justice. We can conclude, even in our sympathies for Plath, that she was wrong. This does not mean that we are merely uncomfortable with her suicide, or that we only mourn. We can praise her brilliant work, and we can say, yes, she was a very good writer, and we can stand in awe of her complex, and intriguing, character. (She did have an authentic voice, as Ted Hughes notes in his introduction to her journals.) And we can continue to read her works and ponder over her too. But we can also criticize her for her last act, even if it was her 'right' to do it.

In this criticism of Plath's ethics, we might note Joyce Carol Oates' "The Art of Suicide." Oates talks of "the suicide who is transfixed by metaphor," an idea that certainly applies to Plath, who often seemed to get her poetic visions and insights mixed up with her real-life problems. Was part of Plath's problem her sense of how good a poet she *could* be? Seemingly, she had little humility; she thought that she should not be bound, like other human beings, to cleaning up baby puke. But did she become so lost in her stream-of-consciousness poetic state that she was not able to come back to reality in order to deal with the mundane? Indeed, the mystic state of creativity is a realm where one is, in some ways, disoriented, like the absent-minded professor, but still, at the same time, one's creativity is clear and focused. It was this non-creative world that Plath could not deal with, especially after a period of intense output; these periods occurred at the end of her life, just as they did after her periods of success before her suicide attempt. It was as if Plath had post-partum depression from finishing her work, or couldn't deal with the dullness of life after a great outpouring of creativity.

Oates says that "the suicide who deliberates over his act . . . rejects our human condition of finitude . . . his self-destruction is a disavowal, in a sense, of what it means to *be* human." I conclude that, in addition, suicide is a denial of the mystery of life, a rejection of the future, whatever the future might hold. For whatever might lie ahead, human beings have a duty to affirm life, to give up notions of total human control. We must, as Camus' Sisyphus did, descend the mountain with joy and continue with our tasks and our struggles. Suicide *seems* as though one is taking control of destiny and yet one is not. Suicide, as Oates says, ends only in "deadness," for suicide is not some kind of creation. Plath's last poem was not a poem at all. And one of Plath's legacies to us is her last *negative* statement.

Like Camus' absurd hero, Plath should have realized that life is a balance between hope and despair, between control and fate. Those who defend Plath's suicide by saying that she did not really mean to kill herself, because a nurse was supposed to arrive on time to save her, are also defending Plath's lack of a clear philosophy. Part of her life was a frenzied attempt to be in total control as besuits her German heritage, and part of her life was a total giving in to fate. Was Plath laboring under the illusion of Kant's categorical imperative, where all important moral points are matters of black and white? What absolute universal law is there that says if a creative soul is to live, the fates will make sure that they do? Plath never learned what was her responsibility to control, and every human being should accept some things as being beyond his or her control. We can be sorry for Plath but we do not have to accept her point-of-view. Life, as Ralph Ellison's Invisible Man says, is to be lived—not controlled. And living, of course, means exerting some control, sometimes much of the time. Despite all of Plath's discipline in her studies and her writing, she was not so disciplined in her life. Or perhaps she was just inept, or immature, at the art of living.

Interestingly, if Plath's last word to us was very dark, since that time women have gone on to say much more positive things. We can only wish that Plath herself might be here to comment on the really fine works of fiction from such writers as Oates, Mary Gordon, Gail Godwin, Joanne Greenberg, Alice Walker, and now a whole generation of women. Perhaps Plath's *The Bell Jar*, however slight a novel as it might be in the future, and as judged against those works that grew out of it and away from it, was really the watershed. And Plath's tragic suicide was the waste land from which contemporary women have, and will, free themselves.

In conclusion, we must go forward. There is no going back — to "Daddy" or to childish ways. Maybe not even back to Hamlet-like equivocation or the American Dream — intellectual indulgences that we cannot afford in the modern atomic world. In this forward movement to positive personal and social goals, women must play a key role. But it remains to be seen whether the creative works of women will be more nurturing and life-oriented as befits their biological role, and whether Plath will be remembered as a woman who was torn by pessimistic, Nietzschean male philosophy, as a woman whose full female identity was never developed. In the long tradition from Sappho to Simone de Beauvoir and current liberated women artists, was the non-motivated destructiveness of Plath, turned by illness on herself, an aberration?

Finally, on the ethics of suicide, it must be noted that suicide is an act, a definite act with very final consequences. Therefore, this act must be looked at differently from some other issues of modern freedoms, or even ideas surrounding the right to die with dignity. Proper, timely death can be an affirmation of the life process. These are the distinctions which the nurturers, and all human beings, must make. If life cannot be easily right or wrong, black or white, it can be a process of thoughtful choices that emphasize the compassionate dignity which humans are capable of. Hopefully, then, the reader will have learned from Plath's art and her life, and thus, *her* tragedy can be other people's salvation.

ESSAY QUESTIONS

1. What is the bell jar?

2. How much is Esther living in her own mental world?

3. How much of Esther's life is caused by fate? Which part?

4. How much of Esther's life is caused by her character?

5. How much of Esther's life is caused by her choices?

6. When and where does Esther lose control?

7. How is this book a wasteland description of women's lives?

8. How is this book a beginning point for women writers?

9. How does The Bell Jar relate to the women's liberation movement?

10. What is the history of electro-shock therapy?

11. What is the psychological explanation for Esther's problems?

12. What are the sociological explanations for Esther's problems?

13. What are the historical explanations for Esther's problems?

14. What are the philosophical explanations for Esther's problems?

15. Why are the Rosenbergs significant to this book?

16. What are the life images in the book?

17. What are the death images in the book?

18. What are the comparable images in other literary works to Plath's bell jar?

19. How do you rate this book as a literary piece? Why?

20. What are the three or four ways to approach the moral dilemma of suicide?

21. What kinds of "landscapes" (Esther's term) do the minor characters create for Esther's world?

22. Who is your favorite character in the novel? Why?

SELECT BIBLIOGRAPHY

ABELSON, RAZIEL and FRIQUEGNON, ARIE-LOUISE. *Ethics for Modern Life.* New York: St. Martin's Press, 1982. (includes St. Thomas Aquinas, "The Sin of Suicide"; David Hume, "The Right of Suicide"; Joyce Carol Oates, "The Art of Suicide.")

ALVAREZ, A. *The Savage God: A Study of Suicide.* New York: Random House, 1972. (includes "Prologue: Sylvia Plath.")

AIRD, EILEEN. *Sylvia Plath: Her Life and Work.* New York: Harper & Row, 1973.

BECKER, ERNEST. *The Denial of Death.* New York: The Free Press, 1973.

BUTSCHER, EDWARD. *Sylvia Plath: Method and Madness.* New York: Seabury Press, 1976.

CAMUS, ALBERT. *The Myth of Sisyphus and Other Essays.* New York: Vintage Books, 1959.

CHERNIN, KIM. *The Obsession.* New York: Harper Colophon, 1982.

DAVISON, JANE. *The Fall of a Doll's House.* New York: Avon Books, 1982.

DE BEAUVOIR, SIMONE. *The Second Sex.* New York: Bantam, 1961.

DURKHEIM, EMILE. *Suicide: A Study in Sociology.* Glencoe, Il.: The Free Press, 1951.

FOUCAULT, MICHEL. *Madness and Civilization: A History of Insanity in the Age of Reason.* New York: Vintage, 1973.

GIFFIN, DR. MARY and CAROL FELSENTHAL. *A Cry for Help.* New York: Doubleday, 1983.

GILLIGAN, CAROL. *In a Different Voice.* Cambridge, Mass: Harvard Univ. Press, 1982.

LASCH, CHRISTOPHER. *The Culture of Narcissism: American Life in an Age of Diminishing Expectations.* New York: Norton, 1979.

MILLER, ALICE. *The Drama of the Gifted Child.* New York: Basic Books (Harper Colophon), 1981.

_____. *For Your Own Good.* New York: Farrar, Straus & Giroux, 1983.

PLATH, SYLVIA. *The Bell Jar.* New York: Bantam, 1971.

_____. *The Journals of Sylvia Plath.* New York: Dial Press, 1982.

_____. *Letters Home.* New York: Bantam, 1975.

_____. *The Collected Poems.* New York: Harper & Row, 1981.

OLSEN, TILLIE. *Silences.* New York: Laurel Seymour Lawrence (Dell), 1983.

RIMM, DAVID C. and SOMERVILL, JOHN W. *Abnormal Psychology.* New York: Academic Press, 1977.

SCHEIDMAN, EDWARD, ed. *Essays in Self-Destruction.* New York: Science House, 1967.

SONTAG, SUSAN. *Illness as Metaphor.* New York: Farrar, Straus & Giroux, 1978.

STURGEON, WINA. *Depression: How to Recognize It, How to Cure It, and How to Grow from It.* Englewood Cliffs, N.J.: Prentice-Hall, 1979.

TROMBLEY, STEPHEN. *All That Summer She Was Mad: Virginia Woolf, Female Victim of Male Medicine.* New York: Continuum, 1982.

WOLITZER, MEG. *Sleepwalking.* New York: Random House, 1983. A novel with a fictionalized poet drawn from Plath and Anne Sexton.

ADDITIONAL READINGS*

BANDLER, RICHARD and GRINDER, JOHN. *Frogs into Princes.* Moab, Utah: Real People Press, 1979.

BRUCH, HILDE. *Eating Disorders.* New York: Basic Books, 1973.

ELLIS, ALBERT. *Humanistic Psychotherapy.* New York: McGraw-Hill, 1973.

FROMM, ERIKA and SHOR, RONALD, eds. *Love, Sex, and Identity.* San Francisco: Boyd and Fraser, 1972.

KINNEY, JEAN AND LEATON, GWEN. *Loosening the Grip.* St. Louis: C. V. Mosby Company, 1978.

LAPLANCE, J. and PONTALIS, J. B. *The Language of Psychoanalysis.* New York: W. W. Norton, 1973.

MILAN, JAMES R. and KETCHAM, KATHERINE. *Under the Influence.* Seattle: Madrona Publishers, 1981.

PINKERTON, PHILIP. *Childhood Disorders.* New York: Columbia University Press, 1974.

RAY, OAKLEY. *Drugs, Society, and Human Behavior.* St. Louis: C. V. Mosby Company, 1978.

ROSEN, R. D. *Psychobabble.* New York: Avon, 1979.

TUBBS, STEWART L. and CARTER, ROBERT M. *Shared Experiences in Human Communication.* Rochelle Park, N. J.: Hayden, 1978.

VERNON, P. E., ed. *Creativity.* Penguin, 1972.

ZIMBARDO, PHILIP. *Shyness.* New York: Jove, 1978.

* *This bibliography of readings in psychology was prepared by Harold Kassel, Registered Clinical Psychologist, Chicago, Illinois, for Cliffs Notes, Inc.*

NOTES

NOTES